ASCENT®
CENTER FOR TECHNICAL KNOWLEDGE

ENOVIA V5-6R2015:
DMU Kinematics

Student Guide
2nd Edition

ASCENT - Center for Technical Knowledge®
ENOVIA V5-6R2015: DMU Kinematics
2nd Edition

Prepared and produced by:

ASCENT Center for Technical Knowledge
630 Peter Jefferson Parkway, Suite 175
Charlottesville, VA 22911

866-527-2368
www.ASCENTed.com

Lead Contributor: Scott Hendren

ASCENT - Center for Technical Knowledge is a division of Rand Worldwide, Inc., providing custom developed knowledge products and services for leading engineering software applications. ASCENT is focused on specializing in the creation of education programs that incorporate the best of classroom learning and technology-based training offerings.

We welcome any comments you may have regarding this student guide, or any of our products. To contact us please email: feedback@ASCENTed.com.

General Disclaimer:

Notwithstanding any language to the contrary, nothing contained herein constitutes nor is intended to constitute an offer, inducement, promise, or contract of any kind. The data contained herein is for informational purposes only and is not represented to be error free. ASCENT, its agents and employees, expressly disclaim any liability for any damages, losses or other expenses arising in connection with the use of its materials or in connection with any failure of performance, error, omission even if ASCENT, or its representatives, are advised of the possibility of such damages, losses or other expenses. No consequential damages can be sought against ASCENT or Rand Worldwide, Inc. for the use of these materials by any third parties or for any direct or indirect result of that use.

The information contained herein is intended to be of general interest to you and is provided "as is", and it does not address the circumstances of any particular individual or entity. Nothing herein constitutes professional advice, nor does it constitute a comprehensive or complete statement of the issues discussed thereto. ASCENT does not warrant that the document or information will be error free or will meet any particular criteria of performance or quality. In particular (but without limitation) information may be rendered inaccurate by changes made to the subject of the materials (i.e. applicable software). Rand Worldwide, Inc. specifically disclaims any warranty, either expressed or implied, including the warranty of fitness for a particular purpose.

Contents

Preface

The *ENOVIA V5-6R2015: DMU Kinematics* student guide focuses on how to create and simulate V5 mechanisms using CATIA products. The course begins with an overview of the mechanism design process and then each step in the process is discussed in depth using lectures and hands-on practices. This course also introduces the concept of converting assembly constraints into kinematic joints. Additionally, this student guide provides an introduction to converting V4 mechanisms to V5 as well as the 3D model method of creating kinematic assemblies.

Topics Covered:

- Kinematic analysis process

- Constraint-based joints

- Curve/surface-based joints

- Ratio-based joints

- Compiling and replaying a simulation

- Swept volumes

- Traces

- Sensors

- Clash detection

- Assembly constraint conversion

- CATIA V4 mechanisms

- Simulation with laws

Note on Software Setup

This student guide assumes a standard installation of the software using the default preferences during installation. Lectures and practices use the standard software templates and default options for the Content Libraries.

This content was developed against CATIA V5-6R2015 Service Pack 1.

Lead Contributor: Scott Hendren

Scott Hendren has been a trainer and curriculum developer in the PLM industry for almost 20 years, with experience on multiple CAD systems, including Pro/ENGINEER, Creo Parametric, and CATIA. Trained in Instructional Design, Scott uses his skills to develop instructor-led and web-based training products.

Scott has held training and development positions with several high profile PLM companies, and has been with the Ascent team since 2013.

Scott holds a Bachelor of Mechanical Engineering Degree as well as a Bachelor of Science in Mathematics from Dalhousie University, Nova Scotia, Canada.

Scott Hendren has been the Lead Contributor for *ENOVIA: DMU Kinematics* since 2013.

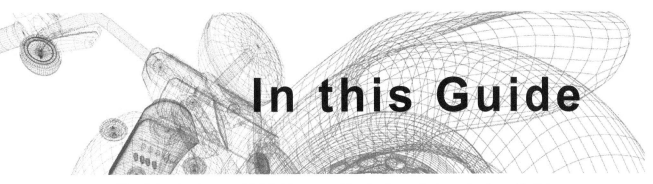

In this Guide

The following images highlight some of the features that can be found in this Student Guide.

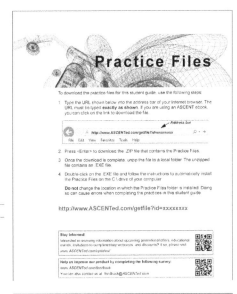

Practice Files

FTP link for practice files

Practice Files

The Practice Files page tells you how to download and install the practice files that are provided with this student guide.

Learning Objectives for the chapter

Chapters

Each chapter begins with a brief introduction and a list of the chapter's Learning Objectives.

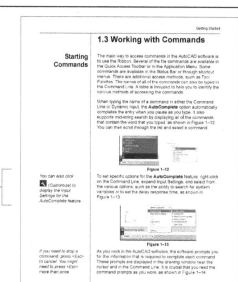

Side notes

Side notes are hints or additional information for the current topic.

Instructional Content

Each chapter is split into a series of sections of instructional content on specific topics. These lectures include the descriptions, step-by-step procedures, figures, hints, and information you need to achieve the chapter's Learning Objectives.

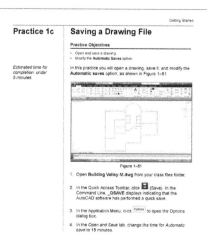

Practice Objectives

Practices

Practices enable you to use the software to perform a hands-on review of a topic.

Some practices require you to use prepared practice files, which can be downloaded from the link found on the Practice Files page.

Practice Files

To download the practice files for this student guide, use the following steps:

1. Type the URL shown below into the address bar of your Internet browser. The URL must be typed **exactly as shown**. If you are using an ASCENT ebook, you can click on the link to download the file.

Address bar

http://www.ASCENTed.com/getfile?id=dendrobatidae

File   Edit   View   Favorites   Tools   Help

2. Press <Enter> to download the .ZIP file that contains the Practice Files.

3. Once the download is complete, unzip the file to a local folder. The unzipped file contains an .EXE file.

4. Double-click on the .EXE file and follow the instructions to automatically install the Practice Files on the C:\ drive of your computer.

    Do not change the location in which the Practice Files folder is installed. Doing so can cause errors when completing the practices in this student guide.

http://www.ASCENTed.com/getfile?id=dendrobatidae

Stay Informed!

Interested in receiving information about upcoming promotional offers, educational events, invitations to complimentary webcasts, and discounts? If so, please visit:

www.ASCENTed.com/updates/

Help us improve our product by completing the following survey:

www.ASCENTed.com/feedback

You can also contact us at: *feedback@ASCENTed.com*

Chapter

1

Introduction to DMU Kinematics

The DMU Kinematics workbench is used to analyze the kinematic motion of an assembly model developed in CATIA V5. Real world motion is simulated by applying joints and commands to a model. Simulations are run by modifying the command through a range of values to drive the motion of the assembly. Here, you are introduced to the process of creating and simulating a mechanism in DMU Kinematics.

Learning Objectives in this Chapter

- Understand the fundamentals of the DMU Kinematics workbench.
- Review the DMU Kinematics interface.
- Understand the Kinematic Analysis process.
- Define a Simulation.
- Run a mechanism analysis.
- Use the Simulation with Commands tool to modify the value of the commanded joint.

1.1 Fundamentals

The CATIA V5 DMU Kinematics workbench assists in the design and analysis of mechanisms. DMU Kinematics enables you to create a virtual mechanism that answers the following questions about a product's design (the mechanism shown in Figure 1–1 is described in these examples):

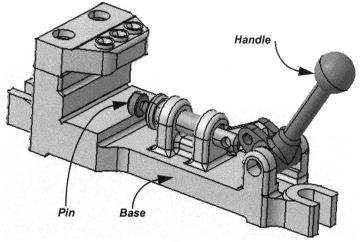

Figure 1–1

1. **Clash Detection:** Are the components of the mechanism going to collide? For example, is the handle going to collide with the base model during operation?

2. **Motion:** Are the components in the mechanism going to move according to the design intent? For example, is there going to be any rotational motion in the pin? Is the system going to lock up at any point throughout the range of motion of the handle?

3. **Velocity and Acceleration:** How fast is the mechanism going to move? Given a specified input rotational velocity at the handle, what be the corresponding linear velocity of the pin going to be?

The information obtained from a kinematic analysis can provide better design alternatives for your mechanism.

1.2 DMU Kinematics Interface

Access DMU Kinematics workbench

To use the kinematic motion analysis functionality in ENOVIA or CATIA, you must access the DMU Kinematics workbench. This is done by selecting **Start>Digital Mockup>DMU Kinematics**.

The workbench symbol changes to .

DMU Kinematics User Interface

The interface for the DMU Kinematics workbench is similar to the other DMU interfaces. The primary differences are the toolbar options that change to **Kinematic** specific tools, as shown in Figure 1–2.

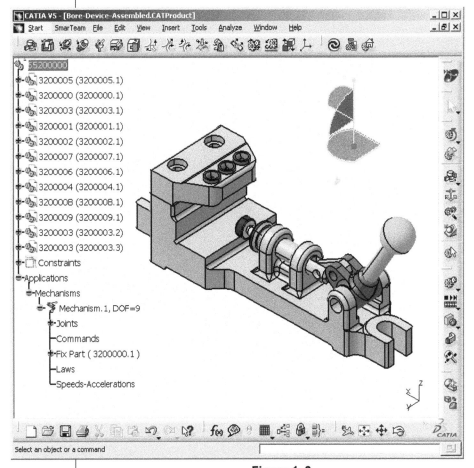

Figure 1–2

1.3 Kinematic Analysis Process

Analyzing a model using DMU Kinematics consists of five main steps:

1. Define a simulation.
2. Perform a mechanism analysis.
3. Run the simulation to test joints and commands.
4. Create a simulation replay.
5. Define outputs.

Each of these steps are described in detail throughout the student guide.

1.4 Defining a Simulation

A simulation consists of the following components:

- **Kinematic Mechanism:** Consists of parts in an assembly. The joints connect each part of the assembly.

- **Fixed Part:** A part that remains stationary while all other parts move in relation to it.

- **Joint:** Defines the type of movement permitted between two or more parts. DMU Kinematics contains seventeen types of joints.

- **Command:** When a joint is commanded, it can be driven by length and/or angle values. As the values change, the joint moves.

General Steps

Use the following general steps to define a simulation:

1. Create a new mechanism.
2. Define a fixed part.
3. Create joint(s).
4. Define a command.

Step 1 - Create a new mechanism.

The first step in defining a simulation is to create a new mechanism. It acts as a storage location for all of the objects of the mechanism in the specification tree. Joints, commands, the fixed part, and anything else related to the mechanism can be found by expanding **Applications** and **Mechanisms** in the specification tree, as shown in Figure 1–3.

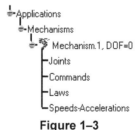

Figure 1–3

To create a mechanism, select **Insert>New Mechanism**. The system automatically adds a **Mechanism.1, DOF = 0** entry to the specification tree.

A mechanism must exist before any other Kinematic entities can be created. You can also create a new mechanism while defining the fixed part (or a joint) by clicking **New Mechanism**, as shown in Figure 1–4.

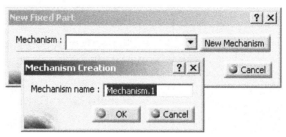

Figure 1–4

It is only necessary to create a single mechanism. Multiple mechanisms can be created to contain a variety of different kinematic setups and analyses. However, a simulation can only run one mechanism at a time.

Step 2 - Define a fixed part.

To put a mechanism into motion, you must define a ground or fixed part to remain stationary while all other parts move in relation to it.

To define a fixed part, click ⚓ (Fixed Part) in the DMU Kinematics toolbar. The New Fixed Part dialog box opens as shown in Figure 1–5, indicating the mechanism in which the fixed part is going to be defined.

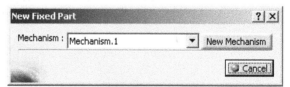

Figure 1–5

To continue the definition, select the part that is going to be anchored. It displays a small anchor symbol and the specification tree displays the part name under the **Fix Part** branch, as shown in Figure 1–6.

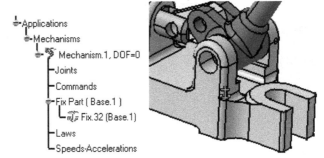

Figure 1–6

Only one fixed part can be defined for a mechanism. If more than one part represents the ground in a mechanism, one of the following operations must be performed:

- Deactivate all other parts that are not going to be in motion.

- Copy all PartBody geometry into one part and remove the source parts from the assembly.

- Create **Rigid** joints between the fixed part and all of the other parts that are not in motion.

Step 3 - Create joint(s).

Other than the fixed part, all of the other parts in the assembly model are free to move anywhere in the reference frame. The reference frame consists of six degrees of freedom: rotation and translation along the X-, Y-, or Z-axes as shown in Figure 1–7.

Figure 1–7

A joint connects two parts and indicates how one part moves in relation to another. Consequently, a joint constrains the relative motion or the degrees of freedom of the two parts.

For example, a **Revolute** joint can be used to define rotational motion, such as a wheel rotating about an axle, as shown in Figure 1–8. Once the joint has been defined, the wheel is only free to rotate about the axis of the axle and is said to have one degree of freedom.

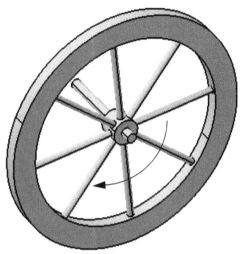

Figure 1–8

To create a **Revolute** joint, click (Revolute Joint) in the Kinematic Joints toolbar. The Joint Creation: Revolute dialog box opens as shown in Figure 1–9.

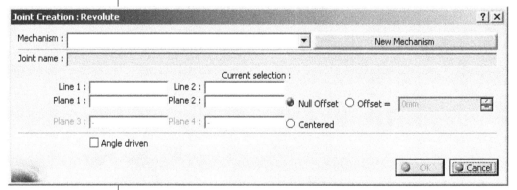

Figure 1–9

You must select each line and plane in the correct order; read the prompts.

Select the required geometry in the correct order. Look for the prompts in the lower left corner of the window. Defining a Revolute joint requires that you select a line and a plane from each model.

The two lines define the axis of rotation. Since no translational degree of freedom is permitted along the axis of rotation, the planes define the relative position of the two models. The planes must be perpendicular to the selected lines. Three options can be used to define the planes:

- **Null Offset:** The planes are coincident.

- **Offset:** The planes are parallel and at a user-defined distance. This distance defaults to the assembled distance.

- **Centered:** Four planes must be selected. Planes 1 and 3 have to be centered between planes 2 and 4, as shown in Figure 1–10.

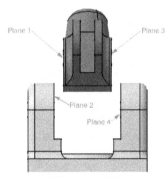

Figure 1–10

Click **OK** to create the joint. The system updates the positions of the two parts according to the selections made for the Revolute Joint. If the model positions do not update, you can do so

manually by clicking ⊚ (Update Positions).

When working in DMU Kinematics in the CATIA interface, you can force the system to automatically update the assembly constraints by selecting **Tools>Options>Mechanical Design> Assembly Design>***General* tab and selecting **Automatic**, as shown in Figure 1–11. This option is not available in the ENOVIA interface.

Figure 1–11

Modifying a Joint

To modify a joint, locate it in the specification tree and double-click on its name, as shown in Figure 1–12.

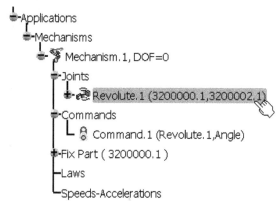

Figure 1–12

The Joint Creation dialog box used to create the joint opens. You can modify any aspect of the joint properties, except the geometry used to define the joint. If the geometry changes, the joint must be deleted and a new joint defined in its place.

Deleting a Joint

To delete a joint, right-click on the joint in the specification tree and select **Delete**. You can click **More** in the Delete dialog box to display additional information, as shown in Figure 1–13.

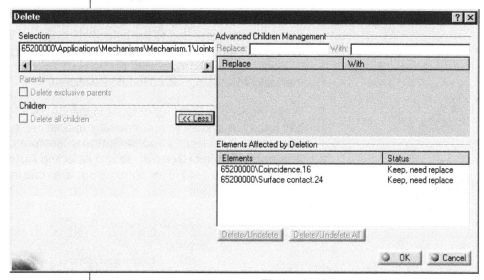

Figure 1–13

Constraint based joints, such as the **Revolute** joint, create assembly constraints. A parent/child relationship exists between the joint and the constraints. The children of the joint are listed in the expanded version of the Delete dialog box. Select any children that should be deleted with the joint and click **OK**.

Step 4 - Define a command.

A command is used to drive the motion of the mechanism by specifying the angle or length values for a joint. At least one joint in a mechanism must be commanded. A joint that is commanded can have its value modified causing the mechanism to move.

To define a command, select **Angle Driven** or **Length Driven** in the Joint Creation dialog box. Depending on the unconstrained degrees of freedom for a joint, you can select angle, length, or both. For example, a **Revolute** joint enables rotation and can only be angle-driven, as shown in Figure 1–14.

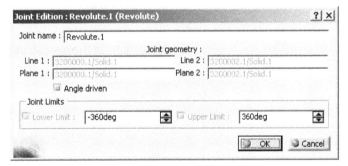

Figure 1–14

Once the mechanism has been completely defined, the Information dialog box opens as shown in Figure 1–15. The mechanism can now be placed in motion.

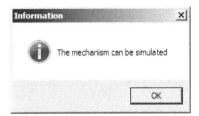

Figure 1–15

Degrees of Freedom

The degrees of freedom of the mechanism must equal zero for it to be simulated by DMU Kinematics. The degrees of freedom can be obtained from the specification tree, as shown in Figure 1–16.

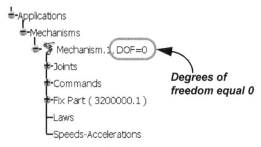

Figure 1–16

If the number of degrees of freedom is greater than zero, verify the following settings:

- Has at least one command been defined?

- Has a fixed part been defined?

- Have enough joints been defined to simulate the mechanism according to the design intent?

1.5 Mechanism Analysis

The Mechanism Analysis is used to confirm that the model is ready to be simulated in DMU Kinematics. To perform a mechanism analysis, click 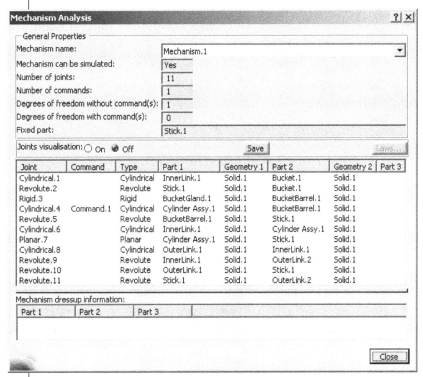 (Mechanism Analysis) or select **Analyze>Mechanism Analysis**. The Mechanism Analysis dialog box opens as shown in Figure 1–17.

Mechanism Analysis ? x

General Properties

Mechanism name:	Mechanism.1 ▼
Mechanism can be simulated:	Yes
Number of joints:	11
Number of commands:	1
Degrees of freedom without command(s):	1
Degrees of freedom with command(s):	0
Fixed part:	Stick.1

Joints visualisation: ○ On ● Off   Save   Laws...

Joint	Command	Type	Part 1	Geometry 1	Part 2	Geometry 2	Part 3
Cylindrical.1		Cylindrical	InnerLink.1	Solid.1	Bucket.1	Solid.1	
Revolute.2		Revolute	Stick.1	Solid.1	Bucket.1	Solid.1	
Rigid.3		Rigid	BucketGland.1	Solid.1	BucketBarrel.1	Solid.1	
Cylindrical.4	Command.1	Cylindrical	Cylinder Assy.1	Solid.1	BucketBarrel.1	Solid.1	
Revolute.5		Revolute	BucketBarrel.1	Solid.1	Stick.1	Solid.1	
Cylindrical.6		Cylindrical	InnerLink.1	Solid.1	Cylinder Assy.1	Solid.1	
Planar.7		Planar	Cylinder Assy.1	Solid.1	Stick.1	Solid.1	
Cylindrical.8		Cylindrical	OuterLink.1	Solid.1	InnerLink.1	Solid.1	
Revolute.9		Revolute	InnerLink.1	Solid.1	OuterLink.2	Solid.1	
Revolute.10		Revolute	OuterLink.1	Solid.1	Stick.1	Solid.1	
Revolute.11		Revolute	Stick.1	Solid.1	OuterLink.2	Solid.1	

Mechanism dressup information:

Part 1	Part 2	Part 3

Close

Figure 1–17

The following questions should be answered using the Mechanism Analysis dialog box:

- Are the degrees of freedom with commands equal to 0?

- What are the number of commands?

- What are the number of joints?

- Is a fixed part defined?

- Can the mechanism be simulated?

1.6 Simulating with Commands

The **Simulation with Commands** tool enables you to modify the value of the commanded joint. As DMU Kinematics plays through these values, the mechanism is placed in motion.

To run a simulation with commands, click 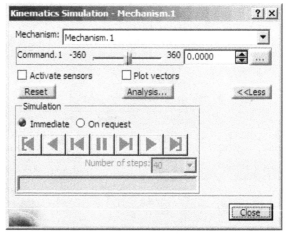 (Simulation with Commands). The Kinematics Simulation dialog box opens as shown in Figure 1–18. If the dialog box does not display exactly as shown in Figure 1–18, click **More**.

*Click **More** to display the VCR controls. Select **On request** to activate the VCR controls.*

Figure 1–18

The current value of the command is shown next to the command name. This indicates the start point for the animation. The end value can be specified by using the slider bar or by entering a new value.

The simulation can be run using the following methods:

- **Immediate:** The mechanism immediately repositions itself to the new command value when it is entered.

- **On request:** The mechanism animates between the current and new command values by clicking ▶. The speed of the animation is controlled by the *Number of steps* value. A large value creates more steps between the start and end values and produce a slower animation.

Click **Reset** to return the mechanism to its original position.

Practice 1a

Create a Mechanism

Practice Objectives

- Create a mechanism.
- Create a fixed part.
- Create a Revolute joint.
- Simulate the mechanism.

In this practice, you will create a simple kinematic mechanism using the wheel assembly shown in Figure 1–19.

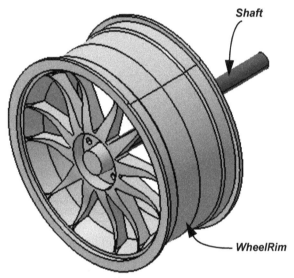

Figure 1–19

The shaft model is defined as the fixed part. A commanded **Revolute** joint will be defined between the shaft and the rim to simulate rotational motion. Once the mechanism has been prepared, it will be simulated.

Task 1 - Open Wheel.CATProduct.

1. Open the assembly model **Wheel.CATProduct**. To quickly locate the assembly, you can expand the Type drop-down list and select **Products (*.CATProduct)**.

The assembly consists of a rim part and a shaft part that have been snapped together. The assembly displays as shown in Figure 1–20.

Figure 1–20

2. Verify that you are in the DMU Kinematics workbench. The workbench symbol should be 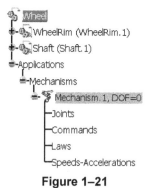. If not, select **Start>Digital Mockup>DMU Kinematics**.

Task 2 - Create a new mechanism.

---

1. Select **Insert>New Mechanism** to build the mechanism structure. A Mechanism entry displays under the **Applications** branch in the specification tree.

2. Expand the **Mechanisms** branch in the specification tree to display the structure, as shown in Figure 1–21.

Wheel
— WheelRim (WheelRim.1)
— Shaft (Shaft.1)
— Applications
— Mechanisms
— Mechanism.1, DOF=0
— Joints
— Commands
— Laws
— Speeds-Accelerations

Figure 1–21

Task 3 - Define the fixed part.

1. Click  (Fixed Part). The New Fixed Part dialog box opens as shown in Figure 1–22.

Figure 1–22

2. Select **Shaft** in the window or specification tree. An anchor symbol displays on the part as shown in Figure 1–23. You might need to zoom in on the part to display the anchor symbol.

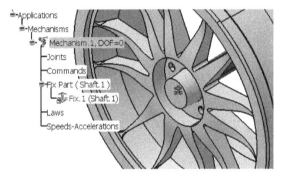

Figure 1–23

Task 4 - Define a Revolute joint.

1. Use the compass to move the two models apart. Since the model is in its assembled position, this will make it easier to select references for the joint. The assembly displays, as shown in the example in Figure 1–24.

Figure 1–24

2. Click 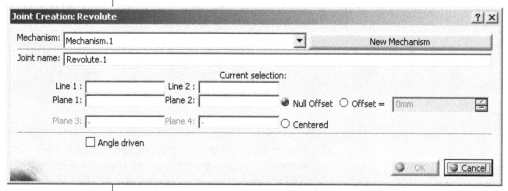 (Revolute Joint). The Joint Creation: Revolute dialog box opens as shown in Figure 1–25.

Joint Creation: Revolute

Mechanism: Mechanism.1 ▼   New Mechanism

Joint name: Revolute.1

Current selection:

Line 1 :   Line 2 :

Plane 1:   Plane 2:   ● Null Offset ○ Offset = [0mm]

Plane 3: [-   Plane 4: [-   ○ Centered

☐ Angle driven

● OK   ● Cancel

Figure 1–25

3. Make the following selections using Figure 1–26 as a guide:

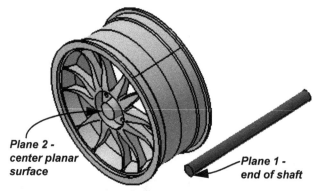

Plane 2 - center planar surface

Plane 1 - end of shaft

Figure 1–26

- *Line 1:* **Select the axis of Shaft.**
- *Line 2:* **Select the center axis of WheelRim.**
- *Plane 1:* **Select the end of the Shaft.**
- *Plane 2:* **Select the center planar surface of WheelRim.**
- *Offset:* **Select this option and enter -8mm.**

4. Click **OK** to complete the joint definition.

5. The shaft model should automatically update to the position defined by the joint, as shown in Figure 1–27. If the model does not automatically update, click 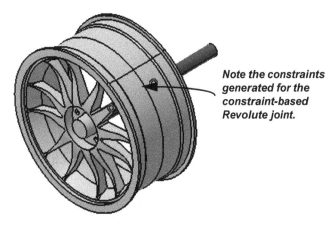 and **OK**.

Note the constraints generated for the constraint-based Revolute joint.

Figure 1–27

Task 5 - Define a command.

This mechanism only has one joint. Redefine the **Revolute** joint by adding an angle-driven command.

1. Expand the specification tree to display the **Revolute.1** joint, as shown in Figure 1–28.

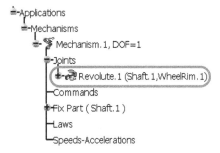

Figure 1–28

2. Double-click on **Revolute.1** to open the Joint Definition dialog box. Note that the *Joint geometry* area is not available. You cannot redefine the geometry used to define a joint.

3. Select **Angle driven** and click **OK**. An Information window opens, as shown in Figure 1–29.

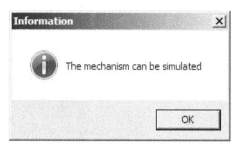

Figure 1–29

4. Note that the specification tree indicates that the degree of freedom for **Mechanism.1** is 0. It is now possible to simulate the mechanism. Click **OK**.

Task 6 - Analyze the mechanism.

1. Select **Analyze>Mechanism Analysis**. The Mechanism Analysis dialog box opens as shown in Figure 1–30.

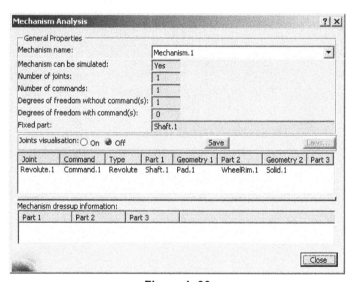

Figure 1–30

2. The Mechanism Analysis is useful for de-bugging problems with a mechanism. In this dialog box, confirm the following information:

- *Mechanism can be simulated:* **Yes**
- *Number of joints:* **1**

- *Number of commands:* **1**
- *Degrees of freedom with commands:* **0**
- *Fixed part:* **Shaft.1**

3. Click **Close**.

Task 7 - Simulate the mechanism.

In this task, you will use the **Simulation with Commands** tool to animate the mechanism. This enables you to modify the value of the command-driven **Revolute.1** joint so that the rim will rotate about the shaft.

1. Click 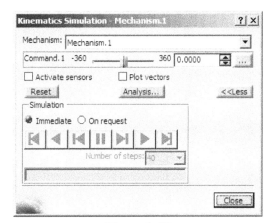 (Simulation with Commands). The Kinematics Simulation dialog box opens as shown in Figure 1–31. If the dialog box opens differently, click **More**.

Figure 1–31

2. Move the dialog box so that the model displays and verify that the **Immediate** option in the *Simulation* field is selected.

3. Slowly drag the *Command.1 slider* to **-360**. As you drag the slider, pause momentarily and watch as the model updates with the new command value.

4. Select **On request**. For *Number of steps*, enter **80**.

5. Modify the Command value to **360**.

6. Click ▶. The model will animate through two complete revolutions (or 720 degrees).

7. Click **Close**.

8. Save the assembly and close the window.

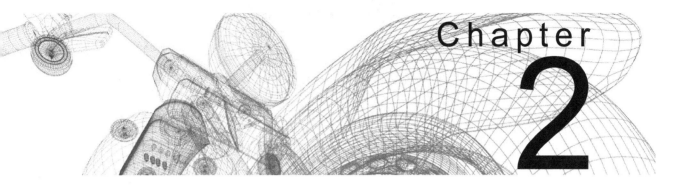

Constraint-Based Joints

This chapter introduces kinematic joints that create assembly constraints between the selected components. Constraint-based joints can develop coincident, offset, and fix together constraints that position the assembly components in both the Kinematic and Assembly Design workbenches. Constraint-based joints enable you to prescribe a variety of types of motion, including rotation about an axis and planar sliding.

Learning Objectives in this Chapter

- Understand constraint-based joints.
- Understand various joint types including Prismatic, Cylindrical, Screw, Spherical, Planar and Rigid joints.

2.1 Constraint-Based Joints

Assembly constraints are generated when certain types of joints are defined. The joints and types of assembly constraints that are generated are described as follows:

Joint type	Constraints
(Revolute)	1. Coincidence between axes. 2. Offset between planes.
(Prismatic)	1. Coincidence between lines or edges. 2. Coincidence between planes.
(Cylindrical)	1. Coincidence between axes.
(Screw)	1. Coincidence between axes.
(Spherical)	1. Coincidence between points.
(Planar)	1. Coincidence between planes.
(Rigid)	1. FixTogether between parts.

2.2 Prismatic Joint

A **Prismatic** joint simulates a linear sliding motion. For example, a block sliding along a linear track would be simulated using a **Prismatic** joint. The joint can slide up and down but cannot rotate, as shown in Figure 2–1.

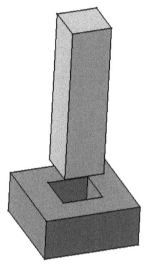

Figure 2–1

How To: Define a Prismatic Joint

1. In the Kinematic Joints toolbar, click 🗎 (Prismatic Joint). The Joint Creation: Prismatic dialog box opens as shown in Figure 2–2.

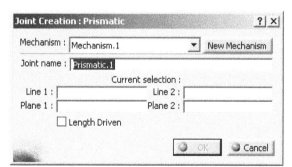

Figure 2–2

2. Define *Line 1* by selecting a line or part edge from the first part.

*Plane 1 and Plane 2
cannot be perpendicular
to the respective line
that was selected.*

3. Define *Line 2* by selecting a line or part edge from the second part. Line 1 and Line 2 become coincident and are connected with an assembly **Coincidence** constraint. The two lines define the direction of the sliding motion.
4. Define *Plane 1* by selecting a part face or reference plane from the first part.
5. Define *Plane 2* by selecting a part face or reference plane from the second part. These two planes are mated and are connected with an assembly **Coincidence** constraint. The two planes define the plane of motion.
6. If the **Prismatic** joint is to be commanded, select **Length Driven**. The length value is defined as the relative distance traveled by the two parts from their assembled positions.
7. Click **OK** to complete the **Prismatic** joint.

2.3 Cylindrical Joint

Cylindrical joints simulate the sliding and rotation motion of a cylindrical part in a hole. A **Cylindrical** joint provides an extra rotational degree of freedom over a **Revolute** joint. An example is shown in Figure 2–3.

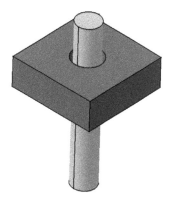

Figure 2–3

How To: Define a Cylindrical Joint

1. In the Kinematic Joints toolbar, click (Cylindrical Joint). The Joint Creation: Cylindrical dialog box opens as shown in Figure 2–4.

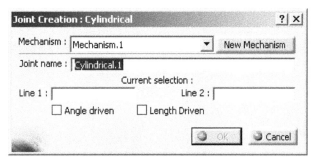

Figure 2–4

2. Define *Line 1* by selecting a line or part edge from the first part.

3. Define *Line 2* by selecting a line, curve, or part edge from the second part. Line 1 and Line 2 become coincident and are connected with an assembly **Coincidence** constraint. The two lines define the direction of the sliding motion.
4. A **Cylindrical** joint can be commanded by angle or length, or both. If the joint is to be commanded, select **Length Driven** or **Angle Driven**. The length and angle values are defined as the relative translation and rotation by the two parts from their assembled positions.
5. Click **OK** to complete the **Cylindrical** joint.

2.4 Screw Joint

A **Screw** joint simulates a screw in a tapped hole. The joint moves up or down as it rotates at a rate equal to the pitch. For example, if the pitch is set to 1mm, then for every 360° the joint revolves it translates 1mm out of the hole. Conversely, for every 1mm the screw is removed from the hole, it needs to rotate 360°. An example of a **Screw** joint is shown in Figure 2–5.

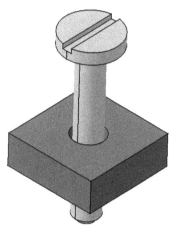

Figure 2–5

How To: Define a Screw Joint

1. In the Kinematic Joints toolbar, click 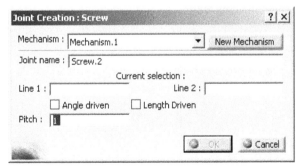 (Screw Joint). The Joint Creation: Screw dialog box opens as shown in Figure 2–6.

Figure 2–6

2. Define *Line 1* by selecting a line or part edge from the first part.

---

3. Define *Line 2* by selecting a line, curve, or part edge from the second part. Line 1 and Line 2 become coincident and are connected with an assembly **Coincidence** constraint.
4. A **Screw** joint can be commanded by either angle or length. If the joint is to be commanded, select either **Length Driven** or **Angle Driven**. The length and angle values are defined as the relative translation and rotation by the two parts from their assembled positions.
5. Enter a value for *Pitch*. The default value is 1 indicating 1mm of translation for every full rotation.
6. Click **OK** to complete the **Screw** joint.

2.5 Spherical Joint

A **Spherical** joint simulates a round ball sitting in a cup. The joint permits a complete 360° of rotation of the center points of the two spheres, as shown in Figure 2–7.

Figure 2–7

How To: Define a Spherical Joint

1. In the Kinematic Joints toolbar, click 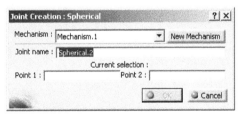 (Spherical Joint). The Joint Creation: Spherical dialog box opens as shown in Figure 2–8.

Figure 2–8

2. Define *Point 1* by selecting a point feature or part vertex from the first part.
3. Define *Point 2* by selecting a point feature or part vertex from the second part. Point 1 and Point 2 become coincident and are connected with an assembly **Coincidence** constraint.
4. Click **OK** to complete the **Spherical** joint.

   You cannot add a length or angle-driven command to a **Spherical** joint. Additional joints and commands must be defined to simulate the mechanism.

2.6 Planar Joint

A **Planar** joint simulates planar sliding motion. For example, a hockey puck sliding along the ice can be simulated using a Planar joint, as shown in Figure 2–9. The joint permits translation in any direction along the plane, but no translation perpendicular to the plane. The joint does permit rotation perpendicular to the plane.

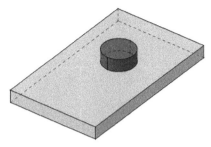

Figure 2–9

How To: Define a Planar Joint

1. In the Kinematic Joints toolbar, click (Planar Joint). The Joint Creation: Planar dialog box opens as shown in Figure 2–10.

Figure 2–10

2. Define *Plane 1* by selecting a part face or reference plane from the first part.
3. Define *Plane 2* by selecting a part face or reference plane from the second part. *Plane 1* and *Plane 2* become coincident and are connected with an assembly **Coincidence** constraint.
4. Click **OK** to complete the **Planar** joint.

   You cannot add a length-driven or angle-driven command to a **Planar** joint. Additional joints and commands must be defined to simulate the mechanism.

2.7 Rigid Joint

A **Rigid** joint simulates two parts that are welded together. When one part is moved, the other part moves as well, as shown in Figure 2–11.

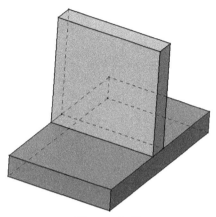

Figure 2–11

How To: Define a Rigid Joint

1. In the Kinematic Joints toolbar, click 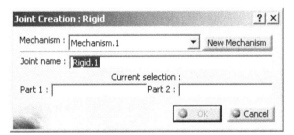 (Rigid Joint). The Joint Creation: Rigid dialog box opens as shown in Figure 2–12.

Figure 2–12

2. Select the two parts that are going to be rigidly connected to define *Part 1* and *Part 2*. An assembly **Fix Together** constraint is created between the two parts.
3. Click **OK** to complete the **Planar** joint.

   You cannot add a length-driven or angle-driven command to a **Rigid** joint. Additional joints and commands must be defined to simulate the mechanism.

Practice 2a

Create a Prismatic Mechanism

Practice Objective

- Create a Prismatic Mechanism.

In this practice, you will create a kinematic mechanism that will simulate a linear sliding motion using the **Prismatic** joint.

Task 1 - Open Prismatic.CATProduct.

1. Open **Prismatic.CATProduct**. The assembly consists of two models, as shown in Figure 2–13.

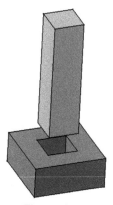

Figure 2–13

2. Verify that you are in the DMU Kinematics workbench. The workbench icon should be ![icon]. If it is not, select **Start> Digital Mockup>DMU Kinematics**.

Task 2 - Create a new mechanism and define the fixed part.

1. Select **Insert>New Mechanism**.

2. Define **Block** as the fixed part.

Task 3 - Create a commanded Prismatic joint.

1. In the DMU Kinematics toolbar, expand the Kinematic Joints flyout and click  (Prismatic Joint). The Joint Creation: Prismatic dialog box opens as shown in Figure 2–14.

Figure 2–14

2. Make the following selections using Figure 2–15 as a guide:

   - *Line 1:* **Select the edge of Square Pin.**
   - *Line 2:* **Select the internal edge of Block.**
   - *Plane 1:* **Select the planar face of Square Pin.**
   - *Plane 2:* **Select the internal face of Block.**
   - Select **Length Driven**.

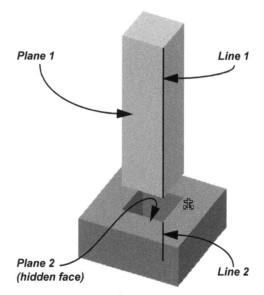

Figure 2–15

3. Complete the joint. It is now possible to simulate the mechanism. Click **OK** to close the information window.

Task 4 - Simulate the mechanism.

1. Click  (Simulation with Commands).

2. Verify that the **On request** option is selected. For the value of *Command.1*, enter **100**.

3. Click ▶ to start the simulation. The square pin comes to a stop at the position, as shown in Figure 2–16.

Figure 2–16

4. Select **Reset**. The mechanism returns to its original position.

5. In the Kinematic Simulation dialog box, click **...**. The Slider: Command.1 dialog box opens as shown in Figure 2–17. Use tit to control the possible range of values for the command.

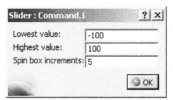

Figure 2–17

6. Specify the following values:

   • *Lowest value:* **0**
   • *Highest value:* **350**

7. Click **OK**.

8. Set *Command.1* to **350** and run the simulation again. The square pin now completely exits the block at the end of the simulation.

9. Close the Kinematic Simulation dialog box.

10. Save the model and close the window.

Practice 2b

Create a Cylindrical Mechanism

Practice Objective

• Create a Cylindrical Mechanism.

In this practice, you will create a kinematic mechanism that will simulate an axial translation and rotation motion using the **Cylindrical** joint.

Task 1 - Open Cylindrical.CATProduct.

1. Open **Cylindrical.CATProduct**. The assembly consists of two models, as shown in Figure 2–18.

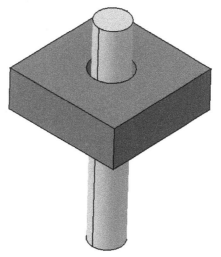

Figure 2–18

2. Verify that you are in the DMU Kinematics workbench. The workbench icon should be [icon]. If not, select **Start>Digital Mockup>DMU Kinematics**.

Task 2 - Define the fixed part and create a new mechanism.

1. Click 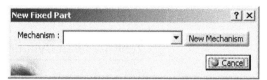 (Fixed Part) to define the fixed part. The New Fixed Part dialog box opens as shown in Figure 2–19. Since a new mechanism has not been defined, the system prompts you to create one on the fly.

Figure 2–19

2. Click **New Mechanism**.

3. Accept the default mechanism name and click **OK**.

4. Define the fixed part by selecting **Block** in the model or the specification tree.

Task 3 - Create a commanded Cylindrical joint.

1. In the DMU Kinematics toolbar, expand the Kinematic Joints flyout, and click 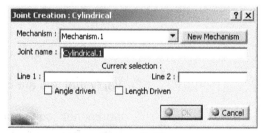 (Cylindrical Joint). The Joint Creation: Cylindrical dialog box opens as shown in Figure 2–20.

Figure 2–20

2. Make the following selections:

   - *Line 1:* **Select the axis of Peg.**
   - *Line 2:* **Select the axis of the hole in Block.**
   - Select **Angle Driven**.
   - Select **Length Driven**.

3. Complete the joint. It is now possible to simulate the mechanism. Click **OK** to close the information window.

Task 4 - Simulate the mechanism.

1. Click 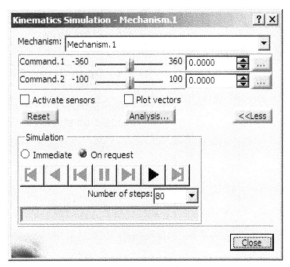 (Simulation with Commands). The Kinematic Simulation dialog box opens as shown in Figure 2–21. Note that there are two commands.

   - The *Command.1* slider controls the angle of the joint.
   - The *Command.2* slider controls the length.

Figure 2–21

2. Verify that the **On request** option is selected.

3. Specify command values so that the peg rotates 360° while translating upwards by 50mm.

4. Play the simulation to confirm that the correct command values have been entered.

5. Click **Reset** to restore the peg position and try different combinations of command values.

6. Close the Kinematics Simulation dialog box.

7. Save the model and close the window.

Practice 2c

Create a Screw Mechanism

Practice Objective

- Create a Screw Mechanism.

In this practice, you will create a kinematic mechanism that will simulate an axial translation and rotation motion using the **Screw** joint. The motion created by a **Screw** joint is identical to a **Cylindrical** joint. However, the joint can only be commanded by angle or length. A pitch value accounts for the other remaining degrees of freedom.

Task 1 - Open Screw.CATProduct.

1. Open **Screw.CATProduct**. The assembly consists of two models as shown in Figure 2–22.

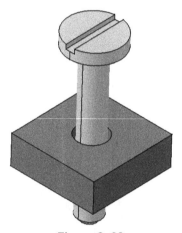

Figure 2–22

2. Verify that the DMU Kinematics workbench is active. The workbench icon should be ![icon].

Task 2 - Define the mechanism.

1. Insert a new mechanism.

2. Define **Block** as the fixed part.

3. Define a **Screw** joint by selecting the axes of screw and the hole in the block.

4. Enter a **Length driven** command for the **Screw** joint.

5. For *Pitch*, enter **10**. The pitch defines the length translated by the screw for every complete rotation. Therefore, the screw translates 10mm for every full rotation.

6. Complete the joint and accept the information window prompting you that the mechanism can now be simulated.

Task 3 - Measure the distance between the screw and block.

In this task, you will measure the distance between the top of the block and the bottom of the screw. This distance will be used to simulate the screw being tightened to the top of the block.

1. Click 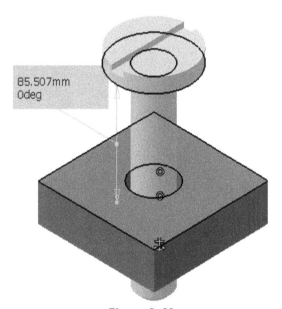 (Measure Between) and measure the distance between the top of the block and the bottom of the screw head, as shown in Figure 2–23.

Figure 2–23

2. Verify that the **Keep Measure** option is selected and close the Measure Between dialog box.

Task 4 - Simulate the mechanism.

In this task, you will use the value of the measurement taken in the last task to drive the command for the **Screw** joint.

1. Click 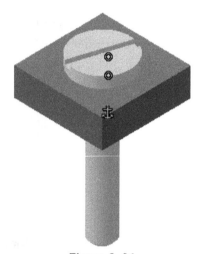 (Simulation with Commands).

2. Verify that the **On request** option is selected.

3. Enter the value of the measurement performed in Task 3 for *Command.1*.

4. Play the simulation. The screw comes to a stop in the position shown in Figure 2–24, but the simulation is too fast to capture it.

Figure 2–24

5. To play the animation more slowly, click **Reset**. In the *Number of steps* field, enter **210**. Play the simulation again.

6. Close the Kinematic Simulation dialog box.

7. Save the model and close the window.

Practice 2d

(Optional) Create a Slide Block Mechanism

Practice Objectives

- Create a multi-joint mechanism.
- Create a multi-command mechanism.

In this practice, you will create a kinematic mechanism consisting of multiple joints and commands. The mechanism consists of two handles, each driving a worm gear that moves a block horizontally and vertically.

Task 1 - Open SlideBlock.CATProduct.

1. Open **SlideBlock.CATProduct**. The model displays as shown in Figure 2–25. The assembly consists of a box, a block, and two worm gears each composed of two components (a fitting and a screw).

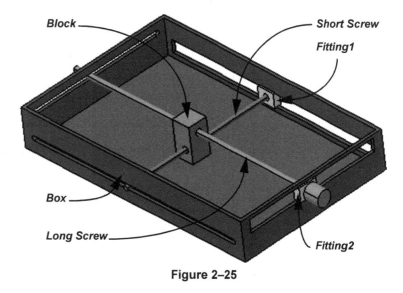

Figure 2–25

Task 2 - Define the mechanism.

1. Insert a new mechanism.

2. For the fixed part, define **Dial** slide box.

---

3. Define the 6 joints as shown in the table below, using Figure 2–25 as a guide.

	Part 1	Part 2	Joint type	Command
1.	Box	Fitting1	Prismatic	
2.	Box	Fitting2	Prismatic	
3.	Fitting1	Short screw	Revolute	
4.	Fitting2	Long screw	Revolute	
5.	Short screw	Block	Screw	Angle driven Pitch = 20
6.	Long screw	Block	Screw	Angle driven Pitch = 20

4. Once all six joints have been defined, reorient the model into the isometric view.

Task 3 - Run simulations on SlideBlock.CATProduct.

1. Click ⬤ (Simulation with Commands).

2. Enter **360** for both commands and simulate the mechanism. The block moves upward and to the left.

3. Close the Kinematic Simulation dialog box.

4. Modify **Screw.5** (controlling the short screw model). For *Pitch*, enter **100**.

5. Modify **Screw.6**. For *Pitch*, enter **150**.

6. Click ⬤ (Simulation with Commands).

7. For *Command.1*, click ⬚. For the *Highest value*, enter **1080**.

8. For *Command.2*, repeat Step 7.

9. Set both commands to **1080** and play the simulation. The final positions of the models display as shown in Figure 2–26. Note that the system continues to simulate the models independent of their positions in the box.

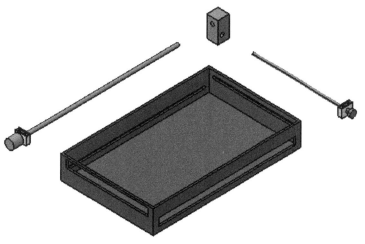

Figure 2–26

10. Save the model and close the window.

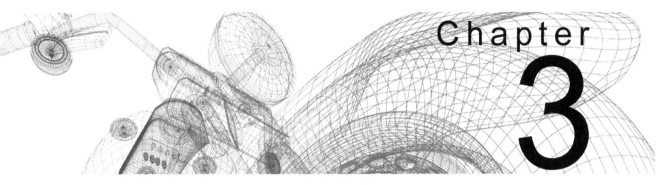

Curve/Surface-Based Joints

Curve/Surface-based joints simulate motion in which a point or curve must follow the path defined by a curve or surface. No assembly constraints are generated during the definition of Curve/Surface-based joints. The joints discussed in this chapter create a connection between a point, curve, or plane from each component. These types of connections enable you to prescribe the sliding or rolling motion created by slot and cam follower mechanisms, as well as rolling objects.

Learning Objective in this Chapter

- Understand the curve-based joints, including Point Curve, Slide Curve, Roll Curve and Point Surface joints.

3.1 Point Curve Joints

Point Curve joints simulate a point following the path defined by a curve. The point is free to translate along the curve and rotate in all three axes. An example is shown in Figure 3–1. To define a **Point Curve** joint, the point must be already positioned on the curve.

Figure 3–1

How To: Define a Point Curve Joint

1. In the Kinematic Joints toolbar, click 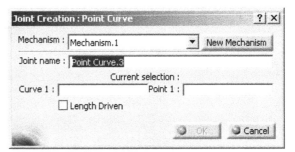 (Point Curve Joint). The Joint Creation: Point Curve dialog box opens as shown in Figure 3–2.

Figure 3–2

2. Define *Curve 1* by selecting a line, curve, or part edge from the first part. The curve can be three-dimensional.
3. Define *Point 1* by selecting a point feature from the second part. The selected point must lie on *Curve 1*.
4. If the **Point Curve** joint is to be commanded, select **Length Driven**. The length value is defined as the distance traveled by the point down the length of the curve.
5. Click **OK** to complete the creation of the **Point Curve** joint.

3.2 Slide Curve Joint

A **Slide Curve** joint simulates one curve sliding along another. For example, a cam-follower arrangement can be created using a **Slide Curve** joint, as shown in Figure 3–3. As the camshaft rotates, the first curve drives the second curve on the valve up and down. The curves must both lie in the same plane and be tangent when the **Slide Curve** joint is defined.

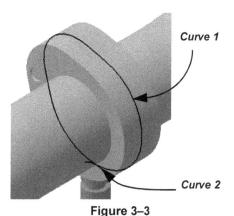

Curve 1

Curve 2

Figure 3–3

How To: Define a Slide Curve Joint

1. In the Kinematic Joints toolbar, click (Slide Curve Joint). The Joint Creation: Slide Curve dialog box opens as shown in Figure 3–4.

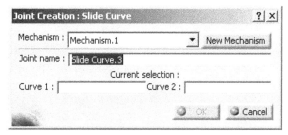

Figure 3–4

2. Define *Curve 1* by selecting a line, curve, or part edge from the first part.
3. Define *Curve 2* by selecting a line, curve or part edge from the second part. The selected curve must be co-planar and tangent to *Curve 1*.
4. Click **OK** to complete the **Slide Curve** joint.
5. A **Slide Curve** joint cannot be commanded. Additional joints and commands must be defined to simulate the mechanism.

3.3 Roll Curve Joint

A **Roll Curve** joint simulates a curve rolling along another curve or line, as shown in Figure 3–5. For example, a wheel rolling on the ground (defined by a curve) can be simulated using a **Roll Curve** joint. The two curves must be co-planar and tangent when the **Roll Curve** joint is defined.

Figure 3–5

How To: Define a Roll Curve Joint

1. In the Kinematic Joints toolbar, click ![icon] (Roll Curve Joint). The Joint Creation: Roll Curve dialog box opens as shown in Figure 3–6.

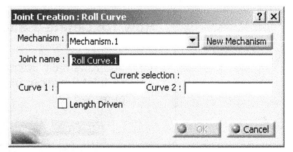

Figure 3–6

2. Define *Curve 1* by selecting a line, curve, or part edge from the first part.
3. Define *Curve 2* by selecting a line, curve, or part edge from the second part. The selected curve must be co-planar and tangent to *Curve 1*.
4. If the **Roll Curve** joint is to be commanded, select **Length Driven**. The length value is defined as the distance traveled down the length of the curve.
5. Click **OK** to complete the **Roll Curve** joint.

3.4 Point Surface Joint

A **Point Surface** joint simulates a point riding on a surface, as shown in Figure 3–7. The joint permits a complete translation and rotation of the point anywhere on the surface.

Figure 3–7

How To: Define a Point Surface Joint

1. In the Kinematic Joints toolbar, click 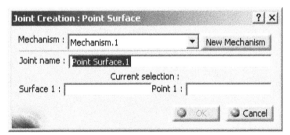 (Point Surface Joint). The Joint Creation: Point Surface dialog box opens as shown in Figure 3–8.

Figure 3–8

2. Define *Surface 1* by selecting a surface or part face from the first part.
3. Define *Point 1* by selecting a point feature from the second part. The selected point must lie on Surface 1.
4. Complete the creation of the **Point Surface** joint by selecting **OK**.

   A **Point Surface** joint cannot be commanded. Additional joints and commands must be defined to simulate the mechanism.

Practice 3a

Slot Follower Mechanism

Practice Objectives

- Create a Point Curve Joint.
- Develop additional joints for a Point Curve mechanism.

In this practice, you will simulate a slot-follower mechanism. This type of mechanism uses a **Point Curve** joint, where the point belongs to the follower model and the curve belongs to the slot model. A **Point Curve** joint only constrains three translational degrees of freedom. Additional joints will be developed to constrain the rotational degrees of freedom.

Task 1 - Open SlotFollower.CATProduct.

1. Open **SlotFollower.CATProduct**. The model displays as shown in Figure 3–9 and consists of three part models: **Ground**, **Slot**, and **Follow**. The **Ground** part model is the fixed part and contains the construction geometry required to define the joints.

Figure 3–9

Task 2 - Set up the mechanism.

1. Create a new mechanism.

2. Define **Ground.CATPart** as the fixed part.

3. Create a **Revolute** joint between **Follow** and **Ground** using the references shown in Figure 3–10. Position the two planes using a null offset.

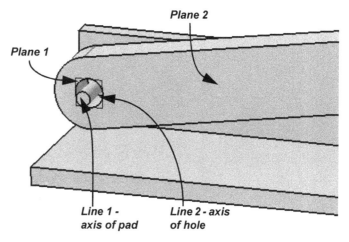

Figure 3–10

4. Create a **Cylindrical** joint between **Slot** and **Ground** using the references shown in Figure 3–11.

*Since the axial translation of **Slot** has already been accounted for by the first **Revolute** joint, a **Cylindrical** joint is used.*

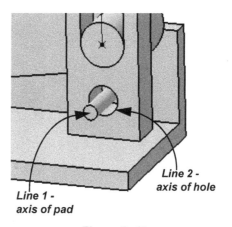

Figure 3–11

Task 3 - Create a Point Curve joint.

1. In the DMU Kinematics toolbar, expand the Kinematic Joints flyout, and click 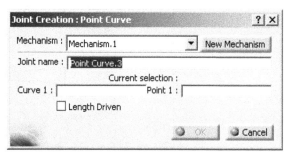 (Point Curve Joint). The Joint Creation: Point Curve dialog box opens as shown in Figure 3–12.

Figure 3–12

2. Make the following selections using Figure 3–13 as a guide:

    *   *Curve 1:* **Select Line.1 from Slot.**
    *   *Point 1:* **Select Point.1 from Follow.**
    *   Select **Length Driven**.

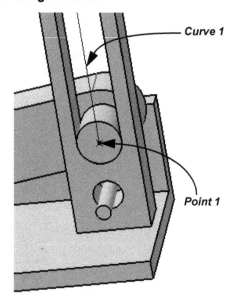

Figure 3–13

3. Complete the creation of the joint and accept the information window prompting you that the mechanism can be simulated.

Task 4 - Simulate the mechanism.

1. Click 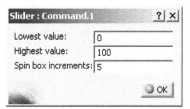 (Simulation with Commands).

2. The slot curve is 100mm in length. For *Command.1*, click **....** In *Lowest value*, enter **0** and in *Highest value*, enter **100**, as shown in Figure 3–14.

Slider : Command.1	? X
Lowest value:	0
Highest value:	100
Spin box increments:	5
	OK

Figure 3–14

3. With the **On Request** option selected, drag the slider for

   Command.1 to **100** and click . As the follower travels along the length of the slot curve, both the **Revolute** and **Cylindrical** joints are rotated. The assembly components come to a stop in the positions shown in Figure 3–15.

Figure 3–15

4. Click **....** For the *Lowest value*, enter **-10**.

5. Drag the slider for *Command.1* to **-10** and play the simulation. Note that although the simulation runs up to a *Command.1* value of -10, the motion of the slot-follower stops at a value of 0, when the point reaches the end of the slot curve, as shown in Figure 3–16. The point of a **Point Curve** joint can never leave the curve to which it was joined.

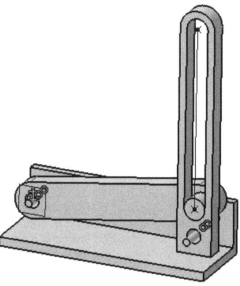

Figure 3–16

6. Close the Kinematic Simulation dialog box.

7. Save the model and close the window.

Practice 3b	# Create a Cam Mechanism

Practice Objective

*   Create a Slide Curve mechanism.

In this practice, you will simulate a cam-follower mechanism. This type of mechanism uses a **Slide Curve** joint, where the profile curve of the cam drives a curve on the follower part. An angle driven **Revolute** joint will be used to generate the rotation of the camshaft.

Task 1 - Open OverheadCamAssy.CATProduct.

1. Open **OverheadCamAssy.CATProduct**. The model displays as shown in Figure 3–17. The assembly consists of three models: **Valve Stem Retainer**, **Camshaft**, and **Valve**. **Valve Stem Retainer** will be the fixed part and consists of two detached solids.

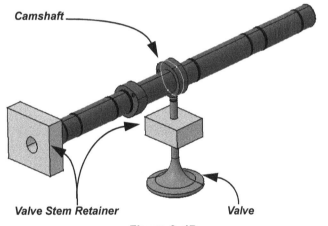

Figure 3–17

Task 2 - Set up the mechanism.

1. Insert a new mechanism and define **Valve Stem Retainer** as the fixed part.

2. Create a **Revolute** joint between **Valve Stem Retainer** and **Camshaft**. Make the following selections for the **Revolute** joint using Figure 3–18 as a guide.

    *   *Line 1:* **Axis of hole in Valve Stem Retainer.**
    *   *Line 2:* **Axis of Camshaft.**
    *   *Plane 1:* **Back face of Valve Stem Retainer.**
    *   *Plane 2:* **Face of Camshaft.**
    *   Select **Null Offset**.
    *   Select **Angle Driven**.

*The **Revolute** joint defines the rotational motion of the camshaft and should be commanded.*

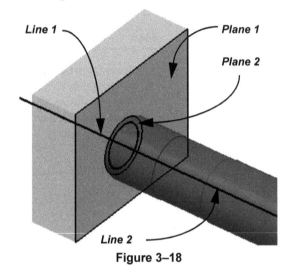

Figure 3–18

3. Close the Information window prompting you that the mechanism can be simulated.

4. Create a **Cylindrical** joint between **Valve Stem Retainer** and **Valve** using the axes shown in Figure 3–19.

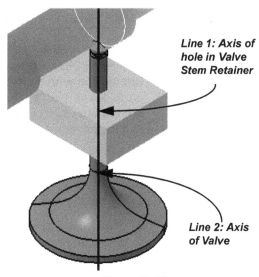

Line 1: Axis of
hole in Valve
Stem Retainer

Line 2: Axis
of Valve

Figure 3–19

Task 3 - Create a Slide Curve joint.

1. In the DMU Kinematics toolbar, expand the Kinematic Joints
   flyout, and click ![icon] (Slide Curve Joint). The Joint Creation:
   Slide Curve dialog box opens as shown in Figure 3–20.

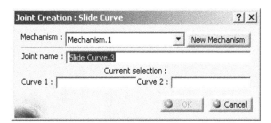

Figure 3–20

2. Make the following selections:

   • *Curve 1:* **The curve on the lobe of the camshaft.**
   • *Curve 2:* **The curve on top of the valve.**

3. Complete the **Slide Curve** joint. The system reports that the
   mechanism can be simulated.

4. Save the assembly.

Task 4 - Simulate the mechanism.

In this task, you will simulate the camshaft mechanism. When simulating **Slide Curve** joints in DMU Kinematics using the **Simulation with Commands** tool, the **On request** option produces very erratic results. For this practice, you will use the **Immediate** option to vary the motion of the camshaft. A solution to this problem is to generate a simulation replay.

1. Click (Simulation with Commands).

2. Select **Immediate**.

3. Slowly drag the slider for *Command.1* between **0** and **360**, and note how the positions of the components update based on the rotation of **Camshaft**. It might take a few seconds for the simulation to catch up with the new command value.

4. Close the Kinematics Simulation dialog box.

5. Save the model and close the window. This model is used in a later practice.

Practice 3c | Roll Curve Joint

Practice Objectives

- Create a Roll Curve joint.
- Develop additional joints for a Roll Curve mechanism.

In this practice, you will simulate a rolling wheel mechanism. This type of mechanism uses a **Roll Curve** joint, where the curve of the wheel rolls down the curve that represents the ground. A commanded **Roll Curve** joint only constrains five degrees of freedom. An additional joint will be developed to constrain the remaining degree of freedom.

Task 1 - Open RollCurve.CATProduct.

1. Open **RollCurve.CATProduct**. The model displays as shown in Figure 3–21 and consists of two part models: **Curve** (which represents the shape of the ground) and **Roll** (which is the wheel model). The **Curve** part model will be the fixed part and contains the construction geometry required to define the joints.

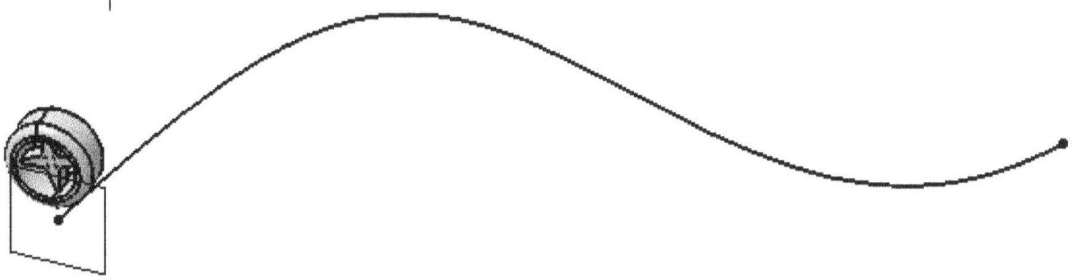

Figure 3–21

Task 2 - Set up the mechanism.

1. Create a new mechanism and define **Curve** as the fixed part.

Task 3 - Define a Roll Curve joint.

1. Click 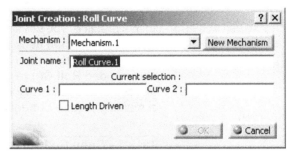 (Roll Curve Joint). The Joint Creation: Roll Curve dialog box opens as shown in Figure 3–22.

Figure 3–22

2. Make the following selections using Figure 3–23 as a guide.

   - *Curve 1:* **Select Sketch.1 from Curve.**
   - *Curve 2:* **Select the edge of Roll that is tangent to Curve 1**.
   - Select **Length Driven**.

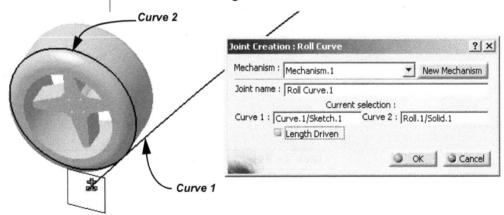

Figure 3–23

3. Complete the creation of the joint. Note that the specification displays one degree of freedom.

Task 4 - Create an additional joint to constrain the degree of freedom.

1. Create a **Planar** joint between **Curve** and **Roll** using the references shown in Figure 3–24.

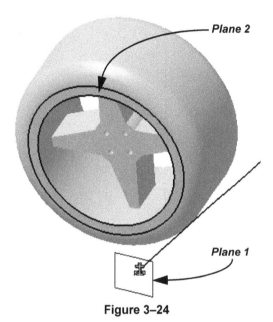

Plane 2

Plane 1

Figure 3–24

2. Complete the joint. The system reports that the mechanism can now be simulated.

Task 5 - Simulate the mechanism.

1. Measure the length of the curve. It is approximately 135mm.

2. Click ![icon](Simulation with Commands) (Simulation with Commands).

3. Modify the lowest and highest values of *Command.1* so that they range between **0** and **130**.

4. Ensure that the **On request** option is selected and set the *Number of steps* to **80**.

5. Play a simulation of the wheel rolling from the start point to the end of the curve.

6. Save the model and close the window.

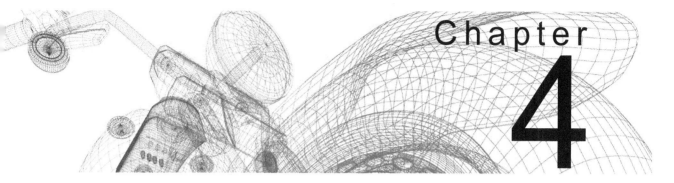

4

Ratio-Based Joints

Ratio-based joints connect two models using a ratio. When the first component is moved, the second component moves at a rate defined by a ratio of the first model's motion. These joints are used to define the motion created by the mechanisms, such as a universal or constant velocity joint, or a rack and pinion mechanism.

Learning Objectives in this Chapter

- Understand ratio-based joints.
- Create ratio-based joints including Universal, Gear, Cable, Rack, Constant Velocity and Axis-based joints.

4.1 Ratio-Based Joints

No assembly constraints are generated during the definition of **Ratio-Based** joints. These joints connect two other joints with a ratio. When one joint is moved, the other joint movement is based on a user-defined ratio. Using two gears as an example, both gears spin on their axes using a **Revolute** joint. These two joints are selected when defining a **Gear** joint. The speed at which gears rotate is based on the ratio specified in the **Gear** joint.

4.2 Universal Joint

Universal joints build a ratio between two **Revolute** joints, called spins, as shown in Figure 4–1.

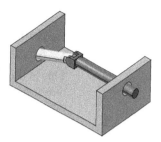

Figure 4–1

As one **Revolute** joint rotates, the other spins at a rate derived from the angle between the two **Revolute** joints. The output rotational velocity of a **Universal** joint varies sinusoidally between a minimum and maximum value. These values can be determined using the following equations:)

MinimumOutputVelocity = cos (α) x InputVelocity

MaximumOutputVelocity = sec (α) x InputVelocity

Where α = the angle between the two spins.

How To: Create a Universal Joint

1. In the Kinematic Joints toolbar, click (Universal Joint). The Joint Creation: U Joint dialog box opens as shown in Figure 4–2.

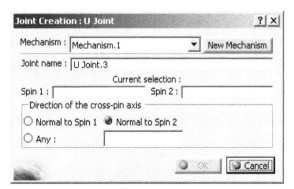

Figure 4–2

2. Select the axis of the input shaft to define *Spin 1*. The input shaft is driven by the commanded **Revolute** joint.

3. Select the axis of the output shaft to define *Spin 2*. The axis or line for *Spin 2* must intersect the axis or line for *Spin 1*.

4. Select an option to define the direction of the cross-pin axis. The options are:

   - **Normal to Spin 1**

   - **Normal to Spin 2**

   - **Any:** Enables you to select any edge or line.

   This is the axis of the cross-pin used to join the two shafts. Its direction is important, since the output shaft rotates at different speeds in different orientations.

5. Click **OK** to complete the joint.

The **Universal** joint cannot be commanded. Instead, the shafts used to define the spins of the **Universal** joint must be connected to the assembly by **Revolute** joints. A command is defined for either of the **Revolute** joints.

4.3 Gear Joint

A **Gear** joint simulates the motion generated by two gears. Each gear is connected to the assembly by a **Revolute** joint. As one gear revolves, the other revolves at a rate defined by the **Gear** joint. An example is shown in Figure 4–3.

Figure 4–3

How To: Define a Gear Joint

1. In the Kinematic Joints toolbar, click (Gear Joint). The Joint Creation: Gear dialog box opens as shown in Figure 4–4.

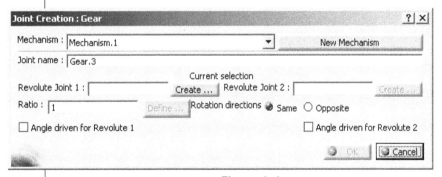

Figure 4–4

2. To define *Revolute Joint 1*, select a **Revolute** joint. This joint can be already in the model, or created on the fly using **Create**.
3. To define *Revolute Joint 2*, select a **Revolute** joint. This joint can also be created on the fly.

4. Enter a value to define the ratio between the two gears. The ratio determines the relative rotational velocity of the uncommanded **Revolute** joint. For example, a ratio of 2 would cause the uncommanded joint to rotate once for every two rotations of the commanded joint.

   The ratio can also be defined based on the size of each gear by clicking **Define**. The Gear Ratio Definition dialog box opens as shown in Figure 4–5. To define the ratio, select the edges of each gear and click **OK**.

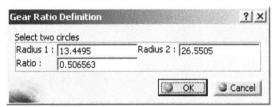

Figure 4–5

5. Specify a rotational direction by selecting either the **Same** (like the gears of a bicycle) or **Opposite** (like a gear set) option.
6. Specify a command for the **Gear** joint. Either **Angle driven for the Revolute 1** or **Angle driven for the Revolute 2** can be selected. This selection overrides any commands specified in either **Revolute** joint.
7. Click **OK** to complete the **Gear** joint.

4.4 Cable Joint

A **Cable** joint is used to drive two **Prismatic** joints, as shown in Figure 4–6. When the commanded **Prismatic** joint moves the other joint also moves based on a user specified ratio. An example of this is a pulley. If you pull down on one side of a pulley system, the object on the other side moves accordingly.

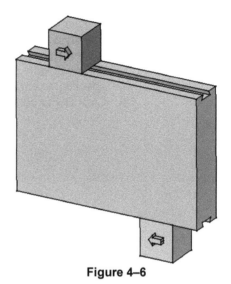

Figure 4–6

How To: Define a Cable Joint

1. In the Kinematic Joints toolbar, click ▦ (Cable Joint). The Joint Creation: Cable dialog box opens as shown in Figure 4–7.

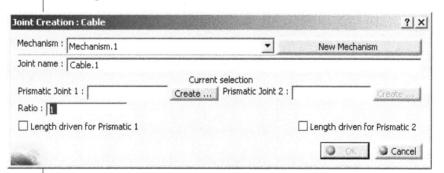

Figure 4–7

2. To define *Prismatic Joint 1*, select a **Prismatic** joint. It can already be created in the model, or can be created on the fly using **Create**.

3. To define *Prismatic Joint 2*, select a **Prismatic** joint. It can also be created on the fly.

4. Enter a value to define the ratio between the two models. The ratio determines the relative speed of the uncommanded joint. For example, a ratio of -2 would cause the uncommanded joint move twice as fast and in the opposite direction to the commanded joint.

5. Specify a command for the **Cable** joint. Either **Length driven for the Prismatic 1** or **Length driven for the Prismatic 2** can be selected. This selection overrides any commands specified in either **Prismatic** joint.

6. Click **OK** to complete the **Cable** joint.

4.5 Rack Joint

A **Rack** joint defines a ratio between a **Revolute** joint and a **Prismatic** joint, as shown in Figure 4–8. When one joint moves, the other moves based on a user-specified ratio. For example, this could be a rack and pinion system used for a steering mechanism of a car. As the steering wheel is turned (using a **Revolute** joint), the rack slides linearly (using a **Prismatic** joint).

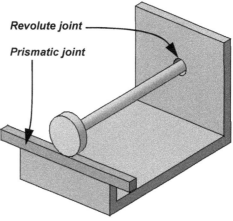

Revolute joint

Prismatic joint

Figure 4–8

How To: Define a Rack Joint

1. In the Kinematic Joints toolbar, click 🖽 (Rack Joint). The Joint Creation: Rack dialog box opens as shown in Figure 4–9.

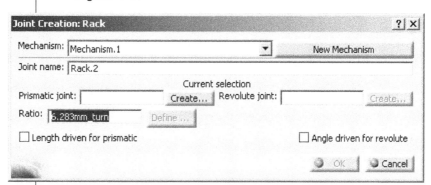

Figure 4–9

2. To define *Prismatic joint*, select a **Prismatic** joint. This joint can already be created in the model or can be created on the fly using **Create**.

3. To define *Revolute joint*, select a **Revolute** joint. This joint can also be created on the fly.

4. Enter a value to define the ratio between the **Revolute** and **Prismatic** joints. The ratio is defined in terms of the distance travelled for each full rotation (e.g. mm/turn). For example, a ratio of 2 (mm/turn) would cause the **Prismatic** joint to move 2mm for every rotation of the commanded **Revolute** joint. In contrast, it would also cause the **Revolute** joint to rotate once for every 2mm of translation from the commanded **Prismatic** joint.

The ratio can also be defined based on the rack and gear by clicking **Define**. The Rack Ratio Definition dialog box opens as shown in Figure 4–10. To define the ratio, select a circular edge on the gear and click **OK**.

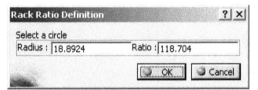

Figure 4–10

5. Specify a command for the **Rack** joint. Either **Length driven for the Prismatic** or **Angle driven for the Revolute** can be selected. This selection overrides any commands specified in either joint.

6. Click **OK** to complete the **Rack** joint.

4.6 Constant Velocity Joint

A **Constant Velocity** (CV) joint consists of three spinning axes. An example is shown in Figure 4–11. The two end shafts spin at the same rate and are connected by a third axis. Each end shaft is connected to the assembly by a **Revolute** joint. The **CV** joint is defined by selecting each axis of the three shafts.

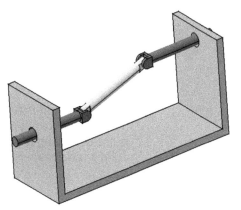

Figure 4–11

How To: Define a CV Joint

1. In the Kinematic Joints toolbar, click 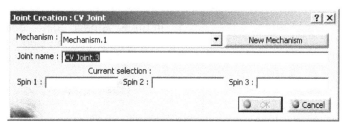 (CV Joint). The Joint Creation: CV Joint dialog box opens as shown in Figure 4–12.

Figure 4–12

2. Select the edge, line, or axis of the three shafts to define *Spin 1*, *Spin 2*, and *Spin 3*. Note that edges, lines, or axes selected for *Spin 1* and *Spin 2*, and for *Spin 2* and *Spin 3*, must intersect.
3. Click **OK** to complete the **CV** joint.

   This joint cannot be commanded and must be driven by either **Revolute** joint connecting *Spin 1* and *Spin 3* to the assembly.

4.7 Axis-based Joint

An **Axis-based** joint permits you to connect two models using a variety of different joint types by selecting an axis system in each model. The following types of joints can be created:

- Universal

- Prismatic

- Revolute

- Cylindrical

- Spherical

An **Axis-based** joint displays in the specification tree using the name of the joint type created. For example, if a **Universal** joint is created using an **Axis-based** joint, it would be displayed as U Joint.1, as shown in Figure 4–13.

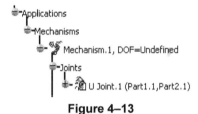

Figure 4–13

How To: Define an Axis-based Joint

1. In the Kinematic Joints toolbar, click ![icon] (Axis-based Joint). The Joint Creation using Axis dialog box opens as shown in Figure 4–14.

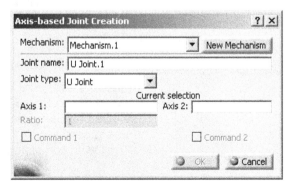

Figure 4–14

2. Expand the Joint type drop-down list and select the type of joint you would want to create as shown in Figure 4–15.

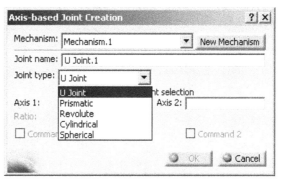

Figure 4–15

3. To define *Axis 1*, select an axis system.
4. To define *Axis 2*, select an axis system from another component.
5. Depending on the type of joint created, you might be able to command the joint. These options are summarized as follows:

Joint Type	Available Command
Universal	None
Prismatic	Length driven
Revolute	Angle driven
Cylindrical	Length and/or Angle driven
Spherical	None

6. Click **OK** to complete the **Axis-based** joint.

Practice 4a

Universal Joint Mechanism

Practice Objective

- Create a Universal Joint.

In this practice, you will create a mechanism to simulate a universal joint. This joint permits rotational motion between two axes (or spins) that are not axially aligned.

Task 1 - Open U_Joint.CATProduct.

1. Open **U_Joint.CATProduct**. The assembly consists of three models: **U Joint Base** and two shafts. **U Joint Shaft 1** is at an approximate angle of 18 degrees from the horizontal.

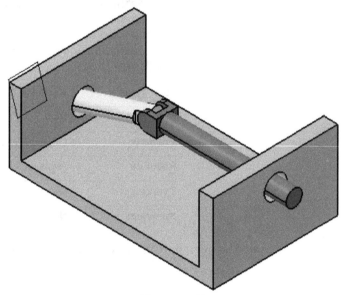

Figure 4–16

Task 2 - Set up the mechanism.

1. Insert a new mechanism and define **U Joint Base** as the fixed part. Create a **Revolute** joint between **U Joint Shaft 2** and **U Joint Base**, using Figure 4–17 as a guide.

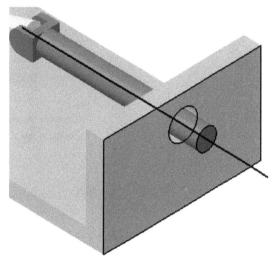

Figure 4–17

2. Select **Offset** and accept the default value. Select **Angle driven** and complete the creation of the joint.

3. Close the information window the prompts you that the mechanism can be simulated.

4. Create a **Revolute** joint between **U Joint Shaft 1** and **U Joint Base** using Figure 4–18 as a guide. Accept the default **Null Offset** option.

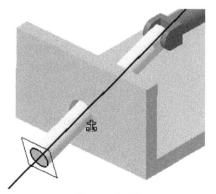

Figure 4–18

Task 3 - Create a Universal joint.

1. In the DMU Kinematics toolbar, expand the Kinematic Joints flyout, and click 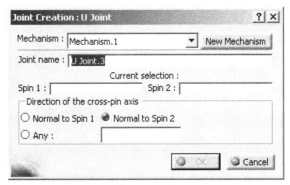 (Universal Joint). The Joint Creation: U Joint dialog box opens as shown in Figure 4–19.

Figure 4–19

2. Make the following selections using Figure 4–19 as a guide:

   - *Spin 1:* **Axis of U Joint Shaft 1**
   - *Spin 2:* **Axis of U Joint Shaft 2**
   - *Normal to Spin 2:* **Accept this default option.**

3. Complete the creation of the **Universal** joint. The system indicates that the mechanism can now be simulated.

Task 4 - Simulate the mechanism.

1. Click 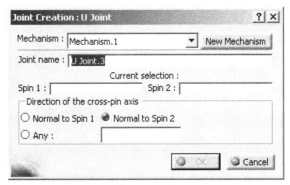 (Simulation with Commands) and enter the following values:

   - *Command.1:* **360**
   - *Number of steps:* **80**

2. Play the simulation.

3. Close the Kinematic Simulations dialog box.

4. Save the model and close the window.

Practice 4b	# Gear Joint Mechanism

Practice Objective

* Create a Gear Joint.

In this practice, you will create a mechanism to simulate the motion developed by a gear pair.

Task 1 - Open GearSet.CATProduct.

---

1. Open **GearSet.CATProduct**. The assembly displays as shown in Figure 4–20 and consists of three models: Table, Spur Gear, and Pinion Gear. Table will be defined as the fixed part while the spur gear will be commanded to turn the pinion gear.

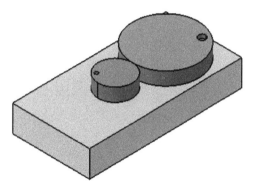

Figure 4–20

2. Using the compass, translate the **Spur Gear** and **Pinion Gear** vertically to the positions shown in Figure 4–21. This will facilitate the creation of the joints.

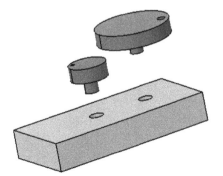

Figure 4–21

Task 2 - Set up the mechanism.

1. Insert a new mechanism and define **Table** as the fixed part.

2. Create a **Revolute** joint between **Table** and **Spur Gear**. Use a **Null Offset** between the top of the **Table** and the underside of the **Spur Gear** to return the gear to its assembled position, as shown in Figure 4–22.

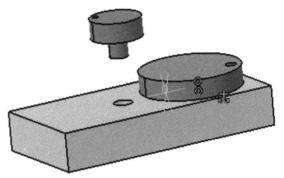

Figure 4–22

3. Create a **Revolute** joint between **Table** and **Pinion Gear**. The model displays as shown in Figure 4–23.

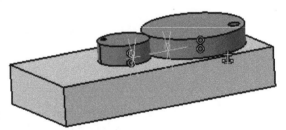

Figure 4–23

Task 3 - Define a Gear joint.

1. Click 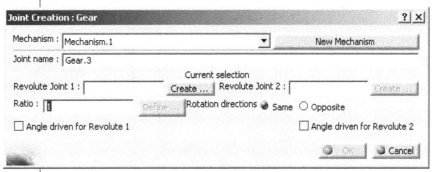 (Gear Joint). The Joint Definition: Gear dialog box opens as shown in Figure 4–24.

Figure 4–24

2. Expand the specification tree to display the joints, as shown in Figure 4–25.

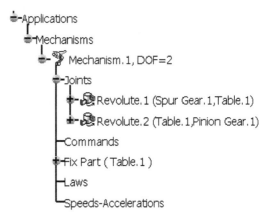

Figure 4–25

3. Make the following selections:

- *Revolute Joint 1:* **Revolute.1**
- *Revolute Joint 2:* **Revolute.2**
- *Ratio:* **2**
- *Rotation directions:* **Same**
- Select **Angle driven for Revolute 1**.

4. Complete the creation of the joint. A **Gear.3** joint is added to the specification tree and the two **Revolute** joints are added beneath the **Gear.3** entry, as shown in Figure 4–26.

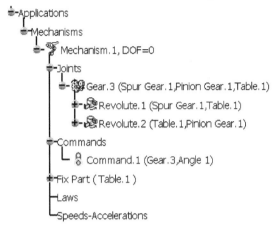

Figure 4–26

5. Close the information window prompting you that the mechanism can be simulated. Simulate the mechanism.

6. Play a simulation of the gears rotating 360°. Note that the **Pinion Gear** rotates at twice the speed as the **Spur Gear**. This is due to the *Ratio* value of 2 being entered during the **Gear** joint definition.

7. Reset the simulation and close the Kinematics Simulation dialog box.

8. Modify the **Gear.3** joint and enter a *Ratio* value of **5**.

9. Replay the simulation, noting the change in speed of the **Pinion Gear**.

10. Reset the simulation and close the Kinematics Simulation dialog box.

11. Modify **Gear.3**. For the *Rotation directions*, select **Opposite**.

12. Replay the simulation noting the change in direction of **Pinion Gear**.

13. Close the Kinematics Simulation dialog box.

14. Save the model and close the window.

Practice 4c | Cable Joint Mechanism

Practice Objective

- Create a Cable Joint.

In this practice, you will create a mechanism that simulates the motion generated by a cable mechanism.

Task 1 - Open Cable.CATProduct.

1. Open **Cable.CATProduct**. The assembly model displays as shown in Figure 4–27 and consists of three models: **Cable block**, **Cable up block**, and **Cable down block**.

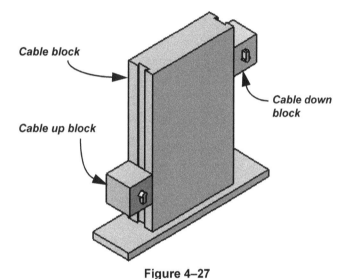

Cable block

Cable down block

Cable up block

Figure 4–27

Task 2 - Create the mechanism.

1. Insert a new mechanism and define **Cable block** as the fixed part.

2. Define a **Prismatic** joint between **Cable block** and **Cable up block**.

3. Define a **Prismatic** joint between **Cable block** and **Cable down block**.

Task 3 - Create a Cable joint.

1. Click 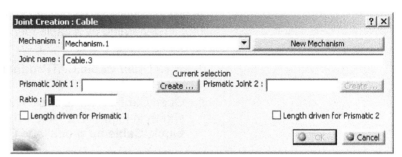 (Cable Joint). The Joint Creation: Cable dialog box opens as shown in Figure 4–28.

Joint Creation : Cable   ? ×

Mechanism : Mechanism.1 ▼   New Mechanism

Joint name : Cable.3

Current selection

Prismatic Joint 1 :   Create ...   Prismatic Joint 2 :   Create ...

Ratio : 1

☐ Length driven for Prismatic 1   ☐ Length driven for Prismatic 2

● OK   ● Cancel

Figure 4–28

2. Expand the specification tree so that the joints display.

3. Make the following selections:

    • *Prismatic Joint 1:* **Prismatic.1**
    • *Prismatic Joint 2:* **Prismatic.2**
    • *Ratio:* **-1**
    • Select **Length driven for Prismatic 1**

4. Complete the creation of the joint. A **Cable.3** joint is added to the specification tree and the two **Prismatic** joints are placed under this entry.

5. Close the information window indicating that the mechanism can be simulated.

Task 4 - Simulate the mechanism.

1. Click (Simulation with Commands).

2. For *Command.1*, enter a value of **65** and play the simulation.

3. Reset the simulation.

4. Experiment with different ratio values for the **Cable.3** joint. After each change, simulate the mechanism to display the results.

5. Save the model and close the window.

<table>
<tr><td>

Practice 4d

</td><td>

Rack Joint Mechanism

Practice Objective

- Create a Rack joint.

In this practice, you will create a mechanism that will simulate the motion generated by a rack and pinion system. This type of system is used to convert rotational motion, such as turning the steering wheel of a car, into translational motion.

Task 1 - Open RackJoint.CATProduct.

1. Open **RackJoint.CATProduct**. The assembly displays as shown in Figure 4–29. The model consists of three parts: **Base**, **Gear**, and **Rack**.

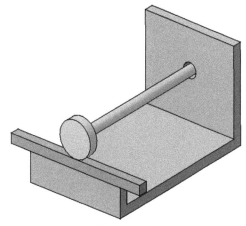

Figure 4–29

Task 2 - Set up the mechanism.

1. Insert a new mechanism and define **Base** as the fixed part.

</td></tr>
</table>

Task 3 - Create a Rack joint.

1. Click 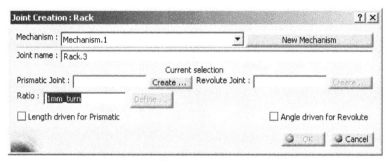 (Rack Joint). The Joint Creation: Rack dialog box opens as shown in Figure 4–30.

Figure 4–30

2. Click **Create** to create a **Prismatic** joint. The Joint Creation: Prismatic dialog box opens.

3. Define a **Prismatic** joint between **Base** and **Rack**. In the Joint Creation: Rack dialog box, the *Prismatic Joint* field is now filled in with Prismatic.1.

4. Click **Create** and create a **Revolute** joint between **Base** and **Gear**.

5. Click **Define** to define a Ratio. The Rack Radius Definition dialog box opens as shown in Figure 4–31. The system prompts you to select a circle.

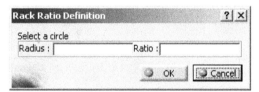

Figure 4–31

6. Select the edge of the gear, as shown in Figure 4–32.

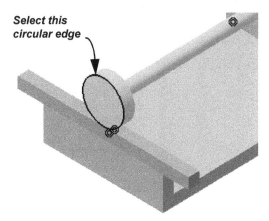

Select this
circular edge

Figure 4–32

The system fills in the dialog box with the values shown in Figure 4–33.

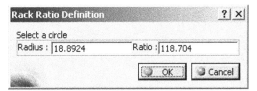

Figure 4–33

7. Select **Angle driven for Revolute** and complete the creation of the joint.

8. Close the information window prompting you that the mechanism can now be simulated.

Task 4 - Simulate the mechanism.

1. Click 🔄 (Simulation with Commands).

2. For *Command.1*, enter a value of **360** and play the simulation.

3. Close the Kinematic Simulations dialog box.

4. Save the model and close the window.

Practice 4e

Create a CV Joint Mechanism

Practice Objective

• Create a Constant Velocity joint.

In this practice, you will create a mechanism to simulate the motion generated by a **Constant Velocity** joint. This type of joint permits eccentricity between the input and output shafts of a mechanism. The output velocity remains the same value as the input velocity.

Task 1 - Open CVJoint.CATProduct.

1. Open **CVJoint.CATProduct.** The assembly displays as shown in Figure 4–34 and consists of four models: **Base** and the three shafts of the constant velocity mechanism.

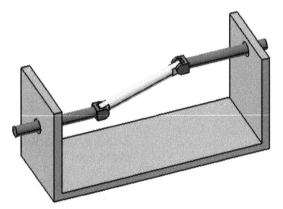

Figure 4–34

Task 2 - Set up the mechanism.

1. Insert a new mechanism and define **Base** as the fixed part.

2. Define the two joints shown below:

Joint type	Part 1	Part 2	Command
Revolute	Shaft 2	Base	Angle driven
Revolute	Shaft 3	Base	

Task 3 - Create a CV joint.

1. Click 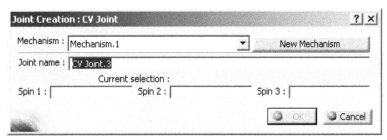 (CV Joint). The Joint Creation: CV Joint dialog box opens as shown in Figure 4–35.

Figure 4–35

2. Make the following selections:

   - *Spin 1:* **Axis of Shaft 2**
   - *Spin 2:* **Axis of Shaft 1**
   - *Spin 3:* **Axis of Shaft 3**

3. Complete the creation of the joint and accept the information window prompting you that the mechanism can be simulated.

Task 4 - Simulate the mechanism.

1. Use the **Simulation with Commands** tool to simulate the mechanism.

2. For *Command.1*, enter **360** and play the simulation.

3. Close the Kinematic Simulations dialog box.

4. Save the model and close the window.

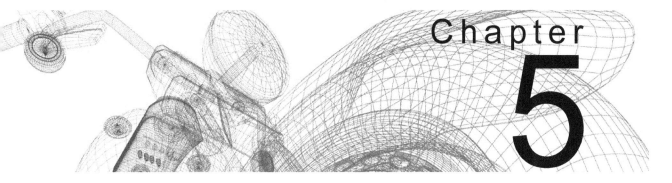

Chapter

5

Simulations

So far, the Simulation with Commands tool has been used to view a kinematic mechanism in motion. This is useful for quickly checking and viewing a mechanism. To store the results of a mechanism analysis, the Simulation tool is used. This simulation is compiled and can be replayed at any time, inside or outside of ENOVIA DMU.

Learning Objectives in this Chapter

- Understand the process of simulating a mechanism.
- Learn how to compile a simulation.
- Learn how to replay a simulation.

5.1 Simulating the Mechanism

The **Simulation** tool is used throughout the DMU workbenches for Fitting, Kinematics, and Navigator. In the DMU Kinematics workbench, it is used to simulate a mechanism so that it can be compiled and replayed both inside and outside of the Kinematics workbench.

A simulation is built by modifying a command value to move the mechanism into a specific position and then inserting this position into the simulation. As multiple positions are inserted, the simulation moves the mechanism from one position to the next. This enables you to bundle a variety of different command values into one smooth animation.

General Steps

Use the following general steps to simulate a mechanism:

1. Access the **Simulation** tool.
2. Specify command values.
3. Insert the positions into the simulation.
4. Test the simulation.

Step 1 - Access the Simulation tool.

Click (Simulation) in the DMU Generic Animation toolbar. Since more than one mechanism can be present in a product, the system prompts you to select the mechanism, as shown in Figure 5–1.

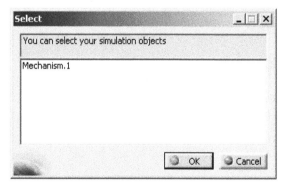

Figure 5–1

Once selected, two dialog boxes open:

- **Edit Simulation:** Used to insert positions into the simulation and replay the results as shown at the top of Figure 5–2.

- **Kinematics Simulation:** Used to modify the command values and reset the positions of the mechanism as shown at the bottom of Figure 5–2.

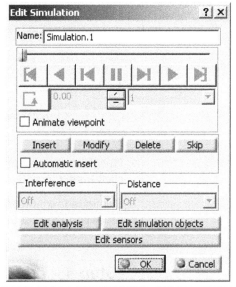

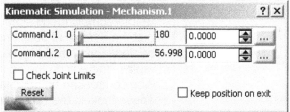

Figure 5–2

Step 2 - Specify command values.

Using the Kinematics Simulation dialog box, enter the corresponding command values for the first position. This is identical to the Simulation with Commands dialog box when the **Immediate** option is selected. The model immediately repositions itself according to the command values entered.

Step 3 - Insert the positions into the simulation.

A simulation is recorded in steps. Each position of the mechanism that is inserted into the simulation creates a new step. The current step displays in the area indicated in Figure 5–3. By default, the position of the model when the simulation is started is inserted at step 0.00.

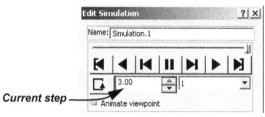

Figure 5–3

Once the mechanism has been placed in the correct position, click **Insert** to add it to the simulation as step 1.00.

Continue to insert steps into the simulation as required by repeating Steps 2 and 3.

Step 4 - Test the simulation.

Before compiling the simulation, it is a good practice to ensure that the order and positions for each step are correct. This can be done using the VCR controls, adjusting the speed of the replay, and editing the sequence of the steps. Additionally, the loop control can be adjusted to repeat or reverse the playback. These tools in the Edit Simulation dialog box are shown in Figure 5–4.

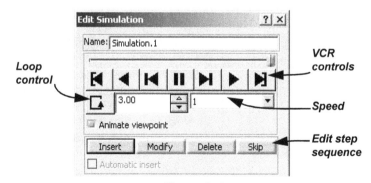

Figure 5–4

5.2 Compiling a Simulation

A simulation is complied to create a replay or simulation file. A replay enables other users who do not have a DMU Kinematics license to view the mechanism in motion. Additional analysis results tools, such as **Swept Volumes** and **Traces**, require replays in order to be displayed. A simulation file (e.g., Microsoft AVI), can be viewed outside DMU using a viewing tool (e.g., Windows Media Player).

General Steps

Use the following general steps to compile a simulation:

1. Access the compilation tool.
2. Select an output format.
3. Define the compilation.
4. Output the replay or simulation file.

Step 1 - Access the compilation tool.

Consider setting up the time step in the Compile Simulation dialogue box, to be low initially. Once you generate a replay, you can only speed up. Your replay can NEVER be at a slower speed.

Click 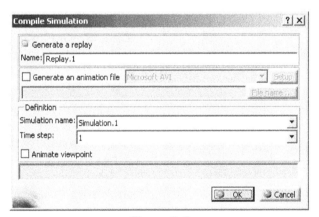 (Compile Simulation) in the expanded DMU Generic Simulation Commands flyout in the DMU Generic Animation toolbar. The Compile Simulation dialog box opens as shown in Figure 5–5.

Figure 5–5

Step 2 - Select an output format.

The simulation can either be compiled as a replay or an animation file.

Replay

How To: Generate a Replay

1. Select **Generate a replay**.
2. Enter a name for the replay.

Animation File

How To: Generate an Animation File

1. Select **Generate an animation file**. The dialog box updates as shown in Figure 5–6.

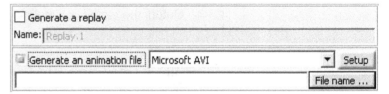

☐ Generate a replay
Name: Replay.1

☑ Generate an animation file | Microsoft AVI ▼ | Setup
File name ...

Figure 5–6

2. Expand the drop-down list and select an option to define the type of animation file generated. Three types of animation files are available:

   • **VFW Codec:** Generates an AVI standard format, which can be viewed in most windows media players.

   • **DirectShow Filter:** Generates an MPG standard format, which can be viewed in most Windows Media Players. MPG offers higher compression and results in a smaller file size than AVI.

   • **Still Image Capture:** Generates an animation, which is viewable on all operating systems. It consists of a series of JPEG screen captures.

3. Click **File name** and enter a filename for the animation file.
4. Click **Setup** to configure the animation file. The Choose Compressor dialog box opens as shown in Figure 5–7.

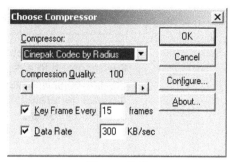

Figure 5–7

This dialog box can be used for the following purposes:

- Select the compressor (or codec) used to compress the file.

- Specify the compression quality.

- Select **Color** or **Black and White** output using **Configure**.

Step 3 - Define the compilation.

The parameters of the compilation are specified in the *Definition* field, as shown in Figure 5–8.

Figure 5–8

How To: Define the Compilation

1. Expand the Simulation name drop-down list and select a simulation.
2. In the *Time step* field, select a value to represent the increment of each step in the replay. A value of 1 results in 1 step per inserted position, and the replay would move quickly. A value of 0.1 breaks each inserted position into 10 steps and results in a slower replay. A value between **0.1** and **0.02** is commonly used. During replay, it is possible to increase the speed of the simulation, but you cannot slow it down. Therefore, you should start with a small time step.

Step 4 - Output the replay or animation file.

Click **OK** to complete the compilation. The simulation plays while it is recorded to a replay or animation file. If a replay was generated, it is added to the specification tree. If an animation file was generated, it can be retrieved from the directory specified in Step 2.

5.3 Replaying a Simulation

Once the simulation has been compiled, it is ready for replay.

This can be done by clicking 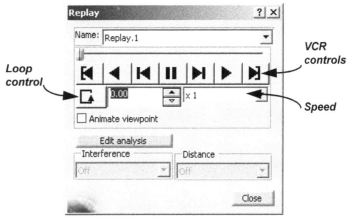 (Replay). The Replay dialog box opens as shown in Figure 5–9. Another method of accessing a replay is to double-click on it in the specification tree.

Figure 5–9

The controls of the Replay dialog box are similar to those in the Edit Simulation dialog box. The replay is started using the VCR controls, and its speed can be controlled using the drop-down list shown in Figure 5–9. The loop control can be used to repeat or reverse the replay.

Practice 5a

Simulate a Mechanism

Practice Objectives

- Create a simulation.
- Compile a simulation.
- View a replay.

In this practice, you will set up and simulate the mechanism shown in Figure 5–10. A simulation is compiled to generate a replay in order to be able to review the specific settings of the simulation at anytime.

Task 1 - Open LinkWheel.CATProduct.

1. Open **LinkWheel.CATProduct**. This assembly consists of four components, as shown in Figure 5–10

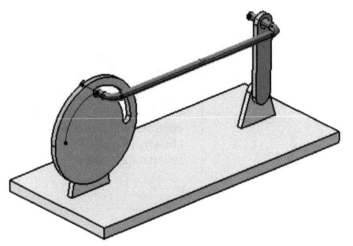

Figure 5–10

Task 2 - Set up the mechanism.

1. Insert a new mechanism and define **Base** as the fixed part.

2. Create a Revolute joint between **Base** and **Link**. Select **Null Offset**.

3. Create a Revolute joint between **Link** and **Rod** as shown in Figure 5–11. Select **Offset** and accept the default value.

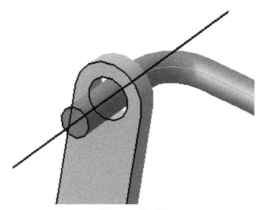

Figure 5–11

4. Create a Revolute joint between **Base** and **Wheel**. Select the **Null Offset** and **Angle driven** options.

5. Modify **Revolute.3** (**Base** and **Wheel**) by double-clicking on it from the specification tree.

6. In the *Joint Limits* field at the bottom of the dialog box, enter the following values:

   - *Lower Limit:* **0deg**
   - *Upper Limit:* **180deg**

7. Create a Point Curve joint between **Wheel** and **Rod**. Select **Length driven**.

8. Close the information window prompting you that the mechanism can be simulated.

9. Modify **Point Curve.4** and enter the following values:

   - *Lower Limit:* **0mm**
   - *Upper Limit:* **56.988mm**

Task 3 - Create a simulation.

1. In the DMU Generic Animation toolbar, click 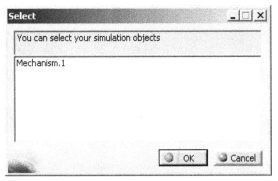 (Simulation). The Select dialog box opens as shown in Figure 5–12.

Figure 5–12

2. In the list, select **Mechanism.1** and click **OK**. The Edit Simulation and Kinematics Simulation dialog boxes open as shown in Figure 5–13.

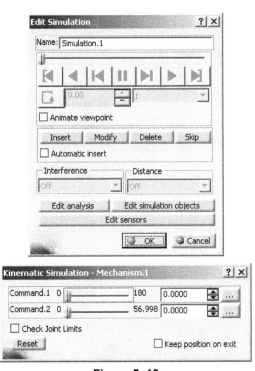

Figure 5–13

3. The system automatically adds the position of the mechanism as the start point for the simulation. For *Command.1*, enter a value of **90** to define the next position in the simulation. The **Wheel** rotates to this new position.

4. In the Edit Simulation window, click **Insert** to insert this position into the simulation.

5. To define the final simulation position, enter the following values in the Kinematics Simulation dialog box:

   - *Command.1*: **180**
   - *Command.2*: **56.988**

6. Click **Insert** to insert this position into the simulation.

Task 4 - Test the simulation.

Once you add the steps to the simulation, it is a good idea to ensure that the replay of the simulation is correct before it is compiled.

1. Expand the drop-down list and select **0.02**, as shown in Figure 5–14. This will slow down the simulation replay.

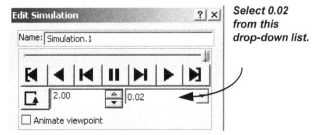

Figure 5–14

2. Click ◀ to play the simulation in reverse from Step 2 to the beginning.

3. If the Rod passes through the wheel then double click on **Revolute.3** from the tree and click on the blue arrow (shown in Figure 5–16), so that the wheel will rotate clockwise.

This can happen if the direction of Revolute.3 is set to rotate counter-clockwise.

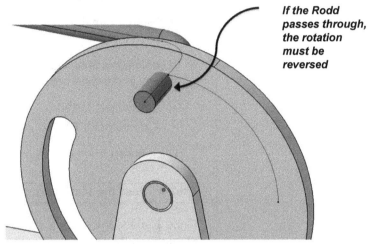

If the Rodd passes through, the rotation must be reversed

Figure 5–15

Click on the arrow to ensure clockwise rotation

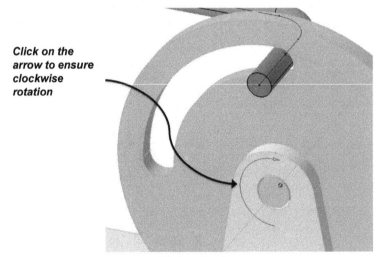

Figure 5–16

4. Click **OK** to finish editing the simulation. A **Simulation.1** entry is added to the specification tree, as shown in Figure 5–17.

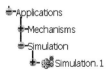

Figure 5–17

Task 5 - Compile the simulation.

In this task, you will compile the simulation. This generates a replay of the simulation so that it can be viewed outside the DMU Kinematics workbench at anytime.

1. Click 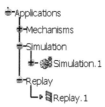 (Compile Simulation). The Compile Simulation dialog box opens as shown in Figure 5–18.

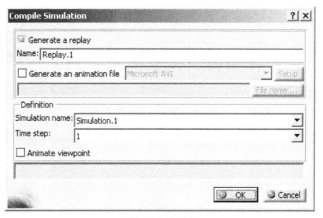

Figure 5–18

2. Ensure that the **Generate a replay** option is selected and accept the default *Name* of **Replay.1**.

3. In the Simulation name drop-down list, ensure that **Simulation.1** is selected.

4. In the Time step drop-down list, select **0.02**.

5. Click **OK**. The progress displays in the dialog box and in the main window as the simulation is compiled.

6. Once completed, a **Replay.1** entry is added to the specification tree, as shown in Figure 5–19.

Figure 5–19

Task 6 - Replay the simulation.

A simulation can be replayed using the **Replay** tool or by double-clicking on the replay in the specification tree.

1. In the DMU Generic Simulation toolbar, click 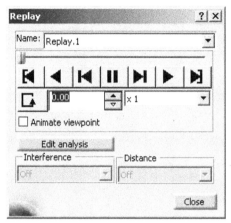 (Replay). The Replay dialog box opens as shown in Figure 5–20.

Figure 5–20

2. In the Name drop-down list, verify that **Replay.1** is selected.

3. Click ▶ to play the animation.

4. Once the animation has stopped, click 🔲 once to change to 🔲. The replay will now loop, playing forward and then backward.

5. Click ▶ to play the animation. The mechanism returns to its starting position and continues to loop through the simulation.

6. At any time, you can click ⏸ to pause the animation.

7. Click **Close**. Note that the mechanism automatically returns to the starting position.

8. Save the model and close the window.

Practice 5b

Simulating the Cam Mechanism

Practice Objective

- Create a simulation.

In this practice, you will work on a cam-follower mechanism. When the **Simulation with Commands** tool was used previously, the system was unable to completely replay the motion due to the complexity of the kinematic equations. You will use the **Simulation** tool to overcome this obstacle.

Task 1 - Open OverheadCamAssy.CATProduct.

If you completed Practice 3b, you set up this mechanism using Revolute, Cylindrical, and Slide Curve joints to simulate the cam follower motion developed by a camshaft. If you completed **OverheadCamAssy.CATProduct**, you can continue to use this model. The files for this practice can be found in the *Completed* directory.

1. Open **OverheadCamAssy_Complete.CATProduct**. The assembly displays as shown in Figure 5-21.

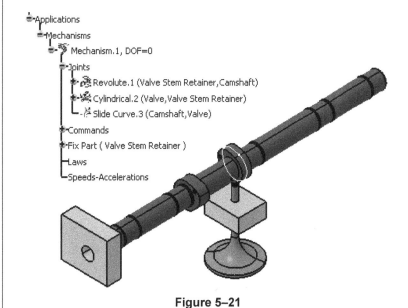

Figure 5-21

Task 2 - Test the mechanism.

1. Click 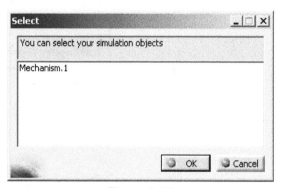 (Simulation with Commands).

2. Select **On request**.

3. For *Command.1*, enter **0** and click ▶. Note that the simulation runs very slowly. It will often stop completely while the command value continues to decrease towards 0.

4. Select **Immediate**.

5. Slowly drag the slider for *Command.1* to **360**. Using the **Immediate** option, the mechanism slowly updates as the command value is changed.

6. Close the Kinematics Simulation dialog box.

Task 3 - Create a simulation.

1. In the DMU Generic Animation toolbar, click
   (Simulation). The Select dialog box opens as shown in Figure 5–22.

Figure 5–22

2. In the list, select **Mechanism.1** and click **OK**. The Edit Simulation and Kinematics Simulation dialog boxes open as shown in Figure 5–23.

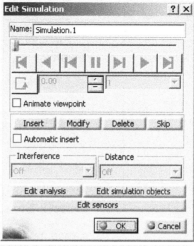

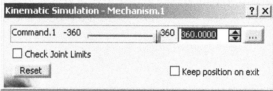

Figure 5–23

3. Drag the slider for *Command.1* to **180**.

4. Click **Insert**.

5. Drag the slider for *Command.1* to **0**.

6. Click **Insert** to create a second step in the simulation.

7. Click **OK** to close both dialog boxes.

Task 4 - Compile the simulation.

1. Click ![icon] (Compile Simulation). The Compile Simulation dialog box opens.

2. Verify that the **Generate a replay** option is selected and accept the default name of **Replay.1**.

3. Expand the Simulation name drop-down list and verify that **Simulation.1** is selected.

4. Expand the Time step drop-down list and select **0.02**.

5. Click **OK** to compile the simulation. This might take a few minutes to complete.

Task 5 - Replay the simulation.

1. In the specification tree, expand **Applications** and expand **Replay**.

2. Double-click on **Replay.1.** The Replay dialog box opens.

3. Click ⬛ twice to permit the replay to loop continuously.

4. Click ▶.

5. Without stopping the replay, expand the drop-down list and select **x 2** to speed up the simulation.

6. Close the Replay dialog box.

7. Save the model and close the window.

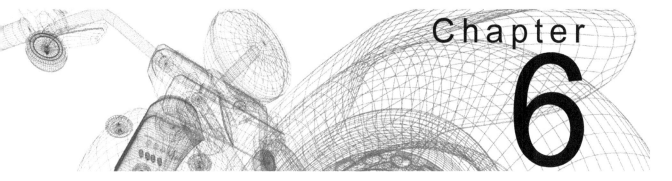

Analysis Results

Once the mechanism has been simulated, a number of tools can be used to extract the resulting data from the motion analysis. These results are used to determine whether the mechanism is functioning according to its design intent.

Learning Objectives in this Chapter

- Understand the process for creating Swept Volumes.
- Create Traces.
- Understand how sensors track specific joint values or measurements as the mechanism is put into motion.
- Use Clash to check for interferences between the different parts of an assembly.

6.1 Swept Volumes

As a kinematic mechanism moves through space, you sometimes need to see the area it moves through. This is useful for clash and clearance detection, and as a visual check that the mechanism is functioning correctly.

This is accomplished by creating a swept volume. The swept volume tool creates a CGR representation of all the positions of the mechanism as it moves through space. An example is shown in Figure 6–1.

Figure 6–1

A replay must be defined before a swept volume can be created. The quality of the resulting CGR is determined by the step size of the replay.

General Steps

Use the following general steps to create a swept volume.

1. Begin the creation of a swept volume.
2. Specify parameters for the swept volume
3. Complete the creation of the swept volume.

Step 1 - Begin the creation of a swept volume.

To create a swept volume, click 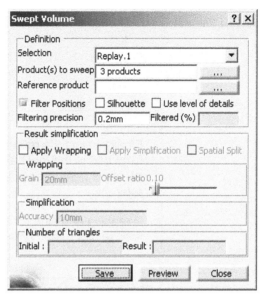 (Swept Volume) in the DMU Generic Animation toolbar. The Swept Volume dialog box opens as shown in Figure 6–2.

Figure 6–2

Step 2 - Specify parameters for the swept volume

Three parameters must be defined to create a swept volume:

*   Replay

*   Product(s) to sweep

*   Reference product

If more than one replay has been defined, select the appropriate replay in the Selection drop-down list.

To define the product(s) to sweep, click **...**. The Product Multiselection dialog box opens as shown in Figure 6–3. Select the required model(s) in the list, using <Ctrl> to select multiple models simultaneously.

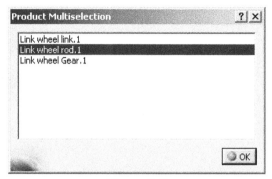

Figure 6–3

Finally, select the reference product using **...**. This is typically the fixed part in the mechanism. The motion of the product(s) to sweep is generated using the reference product as a frame of reference.

Wrapping and simplification are possible if the DMU Optimizer license has been purchased.

Step 3 - Complete the creation of the swept volume.

Once parameters have been specified, the swept volume can be generated. Click **Preview** to display the CGR representation in a separate window. Click **Save** to save the CGR file to the hard drive.

Once the CGR has been saved, it can be inserted into the mechanism by selecting **Insert>Existing Component**. This enables you to visualize the motion of the component in the context of the rest of the assembly.

6.2 Traces

A trace follows the motion of a point in the mechanism through its range of motion defined by the simulation. A new point is generated at each step in the simulation. These points are connected using a spline curve which produces a 3D trace of the motion of the selected point throughout the simulation.

To generate a point trace, a replay generated from a simulation must exist. An example of a trace is shown in Figure 6–4.

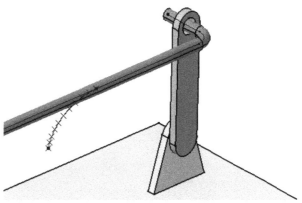

Figure 6–4

How To: Generate a Point Trace

1. In the DMU Generic Animation toolbar, click . The Trace dialog box opens as shown in Figure 6–5.

Figure 6–5

2. Expand the Object to trace out drop-down list and select a replay.
3. Select a point to define the element that is going to be traced. This point is listed in the *Elements to trace out* field.
4. Select a reference product. The reference product is the paper on which the trace is written. Typically, the fixed part is selected. The trace is more useful when taken with respect to a reference that is not moving.
5. Select an option for the destination of the trace. The trace can be created in the selected reference product or placed in a new part model. Placing the trace in a new part model makes it easier to access for hiding or manipulating in the top-level assembly.
6. Click **OK** to complete the trace. The points and curve are created.

6.3 Sensors

Sensors track specific joint values or measurements as the mechanism is put into motion. These values can be graphed and plotted or exported to a file (such as an Excel spreadsheet). An example of a sensor that tracks the distance between two models throughout a simulation is shown in Figure 6–6.

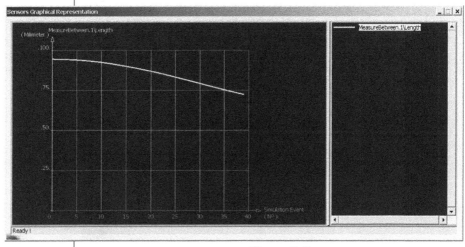

Figure 6–6

It is recommended that you set some parameters before using sensors with a simulation. Select **Tools>Options>General> Parameters and Measure** and select the *Measure Tools* tab. Select the **Automatic update in part** and **Automatic update in product** options, as shown in Figure 6–7. Setting these options enables the measure to be updated as the mechanism progresses through its motion.

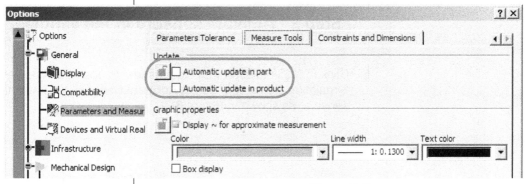

Figure 6–7

General Steps

Use the following general steps to define sensors for your replay.

1. Define a measure to track.
2. Activate sensors in the simulation.
3. Select the sensors to observe.
4. Simulate the mechanism and observe the results.

Step 1 - Define a measure to track.

Click ⬚ (Measure Between) and the **Keep Measure** option to create the measure, as shown in Figure 6–8, which is going to be graphed.

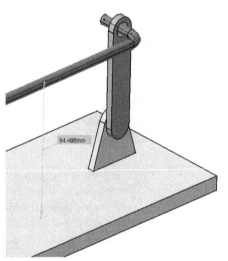

Figure 6–8

Step 2 - Activate sensors in the simulation.

Click ⬚ (Simulation with Commands) to open the Kinematics Simulation dialog box. Select **Activate Sensors** to enable the sensors, as shown in Figure 6–9.

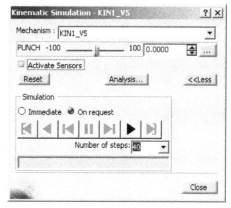

Figure 6–9

When this option is selected, the Sensors dialog box opens. These dialog boxes should be kept open when sensor data is being output.

Step 3 - Select the sensors to observe.

The Sensors dialog box provides a list of all of the joint values and measures that can be observed in the mechanism. An example is shown in Figure 6–10. Selecting a parameter from the list toggles the observed status between observed (**Yes**) and not observed (**No**).

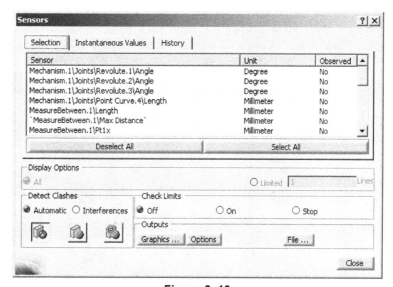

Figure 6–10

Step 4 - Simulate the mechanism and observe the results.

Once you have selected which values to observe, return to the Kinematics Simulation dialog box. Do not close the Sensors dialog box.

Define a simulation by modifying the values of the commands and playing the simulation. The Sensor dialog box must remain open for the values to be observed. Once the simulation is complete, return to the Sensors dialog box to review the results.

The values captured by the sensor can displayed using the options in the *Outputs* field, as shown in Figure 6–11.

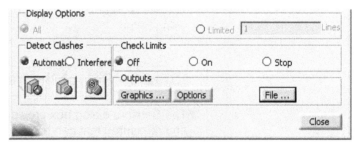

Figure 6–11

Graphical Output

To display a graph of the results, click **Graphics**. The results display in a new window, as shown in Figure 6–12.

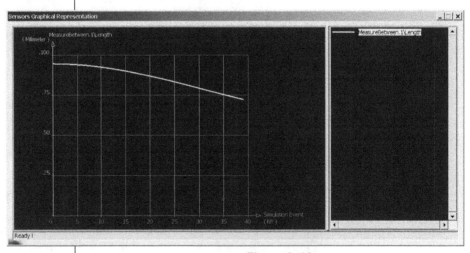

Figure 6–12

Values for specific positions on the graph can be displayed in the bottom left corner by hovering over the required portion of the curve. You can zoom in on specific areas of the graph using the same method used on a 2D drawing.

- To refit the graph to the window, right-click and select **Reframe**.

- You can print the graph by right-clicking and selecting **Print**.

If you are graphing more than one sensor, you must select it from the legend on the right side of the window. This changes the axes to display the correct values for the selected sensor.

File Output

To save the results to an Excel spreadsheet or text file, click **File**. A Save As dialog box opens, enabling you to specify a filename and location. You can save the file as an Excel or Text file.

Instantaneous Values Tab

The *Instantaneous Values* tab displays the parameter value at the current position. This can be used in conjunction with the **Immediate Simulation** option to display sensor results at specific command values. An example is shown in Figure 6–13.

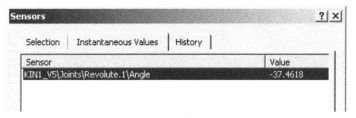

Figure 6–13

History Tab

The *History* tab provides a table that lists the values of the sensor at each step of the replay. An example is shown in Figure 6–14.

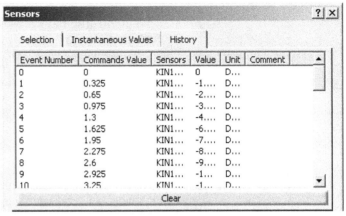

Figure 6–14

6.4 Clash

During simulation, CATIA can check for interferences between the different parts of an assembly. Two methods of clash detection are available:

- Automatic clash detection checks the entire assembly during a Simulation with Commands, Simulation, or Replay.

- The **Clash** tool checks specific models during a Simulation or Replay.

Automatic Clash Detection

Clash can be automatically detected by selecting one of the three icons in the DMU Generic Animation toolbar. The next time the mechanism is simulated, the clash analysis is performed.

The status of automatic clash detection is indicated by the active option in the toolbar, as shown in Figure 6–15.

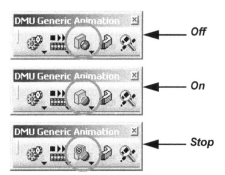

Figure 6–15

The three icons are described as follows:

Option	Description
Clash Detection (Off)	A clash analysis is not performed. This is the default option.
Clash Detection (On)	When the mechanism is simulated, areas of clash detected are highlighted in red.
Clash Detection (Stop)	When the mechanism is simulated, the mechanism stops when clash is detected. The exact stop position is determined by the number of steps entered for the simulation. Higher accuracy is obtained by increasing the number of steps.

Clash Tool

The **Clash** tool enables you to specify which parts of the assembly to check. Clash analysis defined using the **Clash** tool enables specific checks to be made during the simulation. Automatic clash detection analyzes the entire assembly for interference.

There are two steps to performing a clash analysis using the **Clash** tool: defining the clash analysis and adding the analysis to a simulation.

Defining a Clash Analysis

How To: Define a Clash Analysis

1. In the DMU Space Analysis toolbar, click 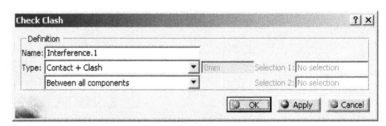 (Clash). The Check Clash dialog box opens as shown in Figure 6–16.

Figure 6–16

2. Define parameters for the clash analysis.

The various clash analysis types are described as follows:

Analysis Type	Description
Contact + Clash	Calculates only contact and clash conditions of the selected components.
Clearance + Contact + Clash	Same as Contact + Clash, but adds a clearance calculation to the selected components
Authorized penetration	Defines a range in which two parts can interfere but not produce a clash result
Clash rule	Uses a Knowledge Rule to calculate clash results

The models involved in the analysis are described as follows:

Selection Type	Description
Inside one selection	Calculates each part in a subassembly against all other parts in the same subassembly.
Selection against all	Calculates each subassembly against all other subassemblies in the current DMU session.
Between all components	Calculates each part against all other parts in the current DMU session. This is the default setting.
Between two selections	Selects a part or assembly to calculate against another part or assembly. The *Selection 1* and *Selection 2* fields become available when this option is selected.

3. Click **OK** to complete the clash definition.

Adding a Clash Analysis to a Simulation

How To: Add a Clash Analysis to a Simulation

1. Modify or create a new simulation. Once in the Edit Simulation dialog box, click **Edit analysis**. The Edit Analysis in Simulation dialog box opens as shown in Figure 6–17.

Figure 6–17

2. Click **Add**. The Select dialog box opens listing the analyses in the model.

3. Select the appropriate clash analysis from the list and click **OK** twice to return to the Edit Simulation dialog box. The *Interference* field in the dialog box is now selectable, as shown in Figure 6–18.

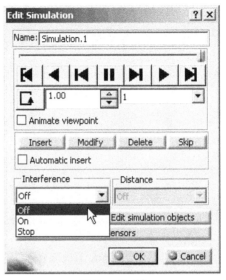

Figure 6–18

4. Expand the drop-down list and select an **Interference** option. These options are identical to the automatic clash detection (**On**, **Off**, or **Stop**).

5. Play the simulation to display the results of the interference analysis.

Practice 6a

Analysis Results

Practice Objectives

- Create a sweep.
- Create a trace.
- Activate and graph a sensor.

In this practice, you will use a replay to analyze the Link Wheel mechanism. You will create a swept volume to determine the spatial claim of the rod. As well, you will use a point trace to determine the trajectory of a point on the rod during simulation. Finally, you will use a sensor to determine how the distance between the rod and base changes throughout the analysis.

Task 1 - Open LinkWheel.CATProduct.

If you completed **LinkWheel.CATProduct**, you can continue to use this model. Otherwise, the files for this practice can be found in the *Completed* directory. In a previous practice, you set up this mechanism using a variety of joints and generated a simulation replay.

1. Open **LinkWheel_Complete.CATProduct**. The assembly displays as shown in Figure 6–19.

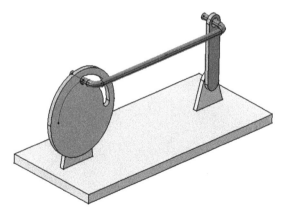

Figure 6–19

Task 2 - Create a swept volume and insert it into the assembly.

1. In the DMU Generic Animation toolbar, click 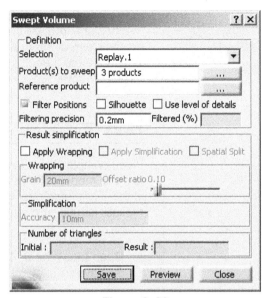 (Swept Volume). The Swept Volume dialog box opens as shown in Figure 6–20.

Figure 6–20

2. Define the Product to sweep by clicking **....** The Product Multiselection dialog box opens. In the list, select **Rod** as shown in Figure 6–21. Click **OK** to continue.

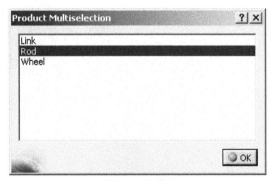

Figure 6–21

3. Click **Preview**. A preview of the swept volume displays in a sub-window, as shown in Figure 6–22.

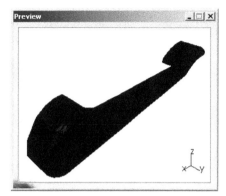

Figure 6–22

4. Close the Preview window.

5. Click **Save**. This produces a CGR (CATIA Graphics Representation) file, which can be inserted into the assembly. Accept the default filename and save the CGR file of the swept volume.

6. Close the Swept Volume dialog box.

Task 3 - Insert a CGR file.

1. In the specification tree, right-click on Link Wheel and select **Components>Existing Component**.

2. Select **Rod_SWEPTVOLUME.cgr** to insert the swept volume into the assembly. The model displays as shown in Figure 6–23.

Figure 6–23

3. Hide the swept volume model.

Task 4 - Create a point trace.

1. In the DMU Generic Animation toolbar, click  (Trace). The Trace dialog box opens as shown in Figure 6–24.

Figure 6–24

2. Make the following selections:

   - *Object to trace out:* **Replay.1**
   - *Elements to trace out:* **Point.3 from Rod**
   - *Reference Product:* **Base**
   - *Trace Destination:* **Reference Product**

3. Click **OK** to generate the trace.

4. In the specification tree, expand **Base**. A new geometrical set has been added to **Base** containing the point trace developed by Point.3 of **Link**. The points display on the model, as shown in Figure 6–25.

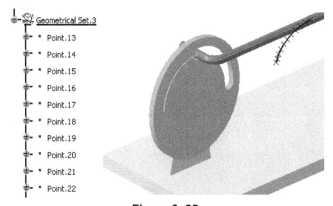

Figure 6–25

5. Hide this geometrical set.

Task 5 - Create a measurement.

1. Click 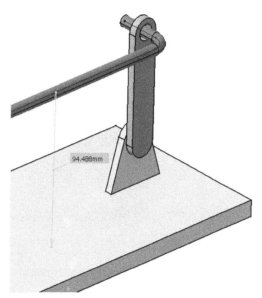 (Measure between).

2. Create a measurement between **Point.3** (used to create the point trace) and the top of the **Base** model, as shown in Figure 6–26.

94.488mm

Figure 6–26

3. Customize the measurement so that only the Minimum distance is measured.

4. Select **Keep measure** and complete the operation.

Task 6 - Define a sensor to measure distance.

1. Click 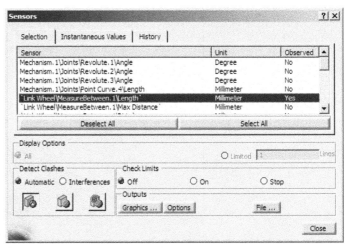 (Simulation with Commands).

2. Select **Activate Sensors**. The Sensors dialog box opens as shown in Figure 6–27.

Figure 6–27

3. In the list of available sensors, select **'Link Wheel\ MeasureBetween.1\Length'**. The observed status will toggle to **Yes**.

4. Switch back to the Kinematics Simulation dialog box without closing the Sensors dialog box.

5. Ensure that **On Request** is selected. For the value for *Command.2*, enter **56.988**.

6. Play the simulation.

7. Once the simulation is complete, click **Graphics** (in the Sensors dialog box) to display the graph shown in Figure 6–28.

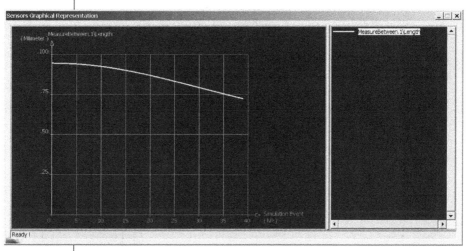

Figure 6–28

8. Hover the cursor over the graphed curve. The current value of the curve displays in a message window at the bottom of the Sensor Graphical Representation dialog box.

*If you zoom in on the graph, you can refit it by right-clicking and selecting **Reframe**.*

9. Hover the cursor over the right end point of the curve. The value of the length parameter at this point is approximately 71.598mm. You might want to zoom in on the graph (using the standard mouse navigation functions from DMU) to get closer to the end of the curve.

10. Close the graph and Kinematics Simulation dialog box.

11. Save the model and close the window.

Practice 6b

Clash Analysis

Practice Objectives

- Automatically detect clashes.
- Perform a Clash analysis.

Task 1 - Open Cable.CATProduct.

If you completed **Cable.CATProduct** in Practice 4c, you can continue to use this model. The files for this practice can be found in the *Completed* directory.

1. Open **Cable_Complete.CATProduct**.

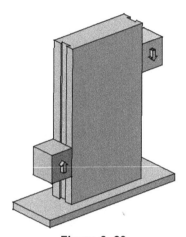

Figure 6–29

Task 2 - Modify the Cable joint ratio.

1. Modify **Cable.3** and enter a *Ratio* value of **-1.5**.

2. Use ![icon] (Simulation with Commands) to simulate the mechanism using a *Command.1* value of **65**. Note that **Down Block** goes through the base of **Cable Block**, as shown in Figure 6–30.

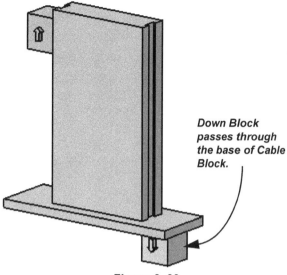

Down Block passes through the base of Cable Block.

Figure 6–30

3. Reset the mechanism and close the Kinematics Simulation dialog box.

Task 3 - Create a replay.

---

1. Click (Simulation). In the Select dialog box, select **Mechanism.1**.

2. In the Kinematics Simulation dialog box, for *Command.1*, enter **85**.

3. In the Edit Simulation dialog box, click **Insert** and **OK** to complete the creation of **Simulation.1**.

4. Compile **Simulation.1** using a time step of **0.04**. **Replay.1** will be added to the specification tree.

Task 4 - Perform automatic clash detection on Replay.1.

---

1. In the DMU Generic Animation toolbar, expand the Clash Detection flyout and drag the toolbar so that it is floating, as shown in Figure 6–31.

Figure 6–31

By default, 📦 (Clash Detection **Off**) is selected so that no clash detection is performed.

2. Click 📦 (Clash Detection **On**) and play **Replay.1**. With clash detection on, the system highlights any areas of clash that are found during the animation. An example is shown in Figure 6–32.

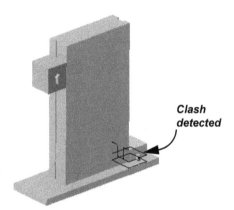

Clash detected

Figure 6–32

3. Reset the replay by clicking ⏮.

4. Click 📦 (Clash Detection **Stop**) and play **Replay.1**. With clash detection set to **Stop**, the replay stops when a clash is found during the animation.

5. Continue to click ▶ to step through the clash. When the clash is no longer detected, the replay continues until it ends or encounters another area of clash.

6. Close the Replay dialog box and click 📦 (Clash Detection **Off**).

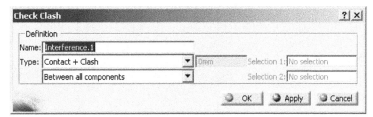

Task 5 - Perform a clash analysis.

1. Click 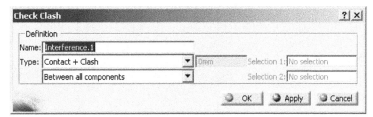 (Clash). The Check Clash dialog box opens as shown in Figure 6–33.

Figure 6–33

2. Accept the default options and click **Apply**. The results of the clash analysis are shown in Figure 6–34. The system detected contact between the two blocks and the base.

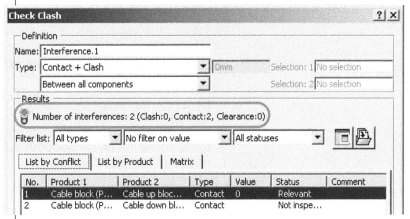

Figure 6–34

3. Click **OK**. An **Interference.1** entry is added to the specification tree.

Task 6 - Simulate the mechanism with clash detection.

1. Edit **Simulation.1**. Note that the *Interference* field in the Edit Simulation dialog box is grayed out. An interference analysis must be selected.

2. In the Edit Simulation dialog box, click **Edit analysis**. The Edit Analysis in Simulation dialog box opens as shown in Figure 6–35.

Figure 6–35

3. Click **Add**, select **Interference.1** from the list, and click **OK** twice to return to the Edit Simulation dialog box. The *Interference* field is now available.

4. Set the *time step* to **0.02**.

5. Expand the Interference drop-down list and select **On**. Play the simulation. When simulating with clash detection, the two models involved in the clash are highlighted.

6. Reset the simulation by clicking ⏮.

7. Expand the Interference drop-down list, select **Stop**, and play the simulation. The simulation stops when interference is detected.

8. Reset the simulation and set the *time step* to **1**.

9. Play the simulation. Note that the interference is not detected. The time step affects the accuracy of when the simulation is stopped.

10. Close all of the dialog boxes.

11. Save the model and close the window.

Chapter 7

Data Reuse

Assemblies are typically created in the Assembly Design workbench, where constraints are applied to locate components relative to each other. These constraints can be converted to constraint-based joints using the Assembly Constraint Conversion tool. This chapter also discusses the use of V4 mechanisms in the V5 DMU Kinematics workbench.

Learning Objectives in this Chapter

- Convert assembly constraints to joints.
- Learn how to replay CATIA V4 mechanisms.

7.1 Assembly Constraint Conversion

Some joints create assembly constraints. The opposite of this process is to create joints from assembly constraints. The **Assembly Constraint Conversion** tool enables you to create a kinematic mechanism from a constrained assembly.

General Steps

Use the following general steps to convert assembly constraints to kinematic joints:

1. Begin the assembly constraints conversion.
2. Define a new mechanism.
3. Define the fixed part.
4. Convert the constraints by pair.
5. Modify or add constraints as required.

Step 1 - Begin the assembly constraints conversion.

With the assembly open in the CATIA DMU Kinematics

workbench, click ![icon] (Assembly Constraints Conversion) in the DMU Kinematics toolbar. The Assembly Constraints Conversion dialog box opens as shown in Figure 7–1.

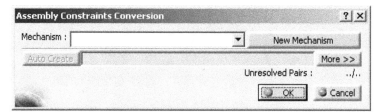

Figure 7–1

Step 2 - Define a new mechanism.

Since a new mechanism is going to be created using the existing assembly constraints, click **New Mechanism** and enter an appropriate mechanism name, as shown in Figure 7–2.

Figure 7–2

Once the mechanism has been created, the Assembly Constraints Conversion dialog box displays the number of unresolved pairs of models. Each constraint connects two models, referred to as a pair. For each pair, any number of constraints can be converted into a kinematic joint between the pair.

Step 3 - Define the fixed part.

To define the fixed part for the mechanism, you must expand the Assembly Constraints Conversion dialog box by clicking **More**. The Assembly Constraints Conversion dialog box opens as shown in Figure 7–3.

Pair of components

Constraints for pair to be converted to a joint

Fixed part definition

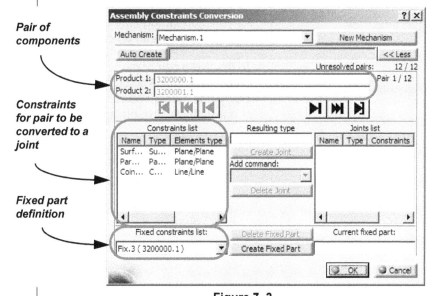

Figure 7–3

All of the fixed constraints are listed at the bottom of the dialog box. To define the fixed part, select a fix constraint (and corresponding model) in the Fix Constraint List dialog box and click **Create Fixed Part**.

To change or delete the current fixed part, click **Delete Fixed Part**.

Step 4 - Convert the constraints by pair.

Be aware that the goal of this process is not to simply convert each constraint set into the corresponding kinematic joint. This can be done by clicking **Auto Create**. Instead, you need to step through each pair of models and determine what type of joint should be developed between the two models.

To step through the pairs of models under consideration, use the player buttons in the dialog box, as shown in Figure 7–4.

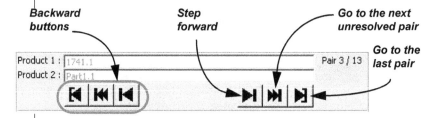

Figure 7–4

As you step through the list of pairs, the corresponding models highlight in the main window.

To resolve a pair of models, select the required constraints in the list using <Ctrl>. The corresponding joint type is listed in the dialog box. As you select the constraints for a given pair, the type of possible joint changes as shown in Figure 7–5.

The selection of a Line/Line constraint yields a Cylindrical joint.

The selection of a Line/Line and Plane/Plane constraint yields a Revolute joint.

The selection of all three constraints fully constrain the model and yield a Rigid joint.

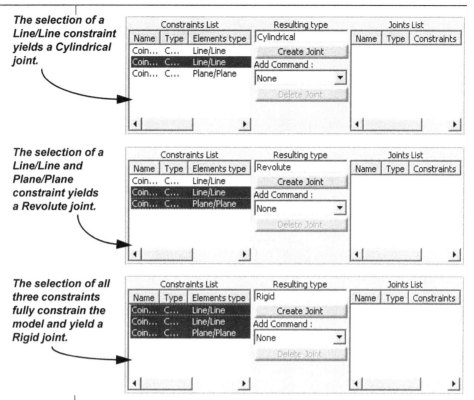

Figure 7–5

If available, a joint can be defined as commanded by selecting **Length** or **Angle** in the Add Command drop-down list.

At any point, you can create the required joint by clicking **Create Joint**. Continue to step through the pairs until the number of unresolved pairs is zero or all required joints have been created.

In some cases, the assembly might have unwanted degrees of freedom. For example, two constraints are typically used when constraining a pin in a hole: axial coincidence and contact. This leaves a rotational degree of freedom about the axis of the pin. Although this pin is intended to be rigidly attached, the Assembly Constraint Conversion tool tries to create a **Revolute** joint (as a result of a line/line and a plane/plane constraint). In this case, it is best to skip the pair and make a **Rigid** joint later.

Step 5 - Modify or add constraints as required.

After the mechanism has been developed using the **Assembly Constraint Conversion** tool, use the **Mechanism Analysis** tool to see what might be required to complete the mechanism (recommended). To perform a mechanism analysis, click

 (Mechanism Analysis).

The assembly might have been constrained in a way that results in a less than optimal mechanism. It is often necessary to modify the joints that were created, add additional joints (such as rigid), or add additional commands. The intent is to reduce the number of degrees of freedom to zero so that the mechanism can be simulated.

7.2 CATIA V4 Mechanisms

Kinematic mechanisms that were created in CATIA V4 can be replayed in ENOVIA V5 DMU Kinematics. It is necessary for the V4 mechanism to be created using the Stick Model methodology.

The Stick Model methodology is a V4 design method, in which the kinematic data for the mechanism is stored in a separate model. This model only contains the geometry required to create the joints of the mechanism: typically lines, curves, and points. The geometry for each part (solid or surface) is stored in its own model. The models are connected to the kinematics using sessions and dressup.

General Steps

Use the following general steps to bring a V4 mechanism into V5:

1. Place the V4 data into a V5 assembly.
2. Copy and paste the kinematic data.
3. Link models to the kinematic data.

Step 1 - Place the V4 data into a V5 assembly.

To play a V4 mechanism, you must first place the V4 models, including the one containing the kinematics, in a V5 assembly. This can be done by creating a new product (**File>New> Product**), and selecting **Insert>Existing Component** to bring each model into the V5 assembly. An example is shown in , where the last model in the tree contains the V4 kinematic data (under KIN1).

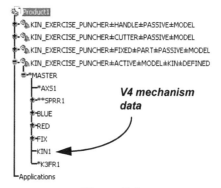

Figure 7–6

Step 2 - Copy and paste the kinematic data.

Expand the V4 model containing the kinematic data in the specification tree until you locate the mechanism entry. An example is shown in Figure 7–7 where the mechanism is named **KIN1**.

Right-click on this entry and select **Copy**. Then right-click on the **Applications** entry in the tree and select **Paste**. This copies all of the information about the V4 mechanism into the V5 product. The result of the **Copy/Paste** operation is shown in Figure 7–7.

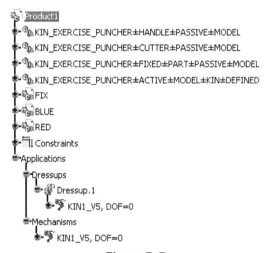

Figure 7–7

Several entries have been added to the product. A model is created for each component of the V4 stick model. Additionally, a **Dressup** and **Mechanism** entry are added. Note that the **Dressup** entry consists of the mechanism, which has been renamed to **KIN1_V5** to indicate its conversion.

The V4 stick model mechanism can now be played in V5. The next step is to link the 3D models in the V5 assembly to the stick models of the kinematic mechanism.

Step 3 - Link models to the kinematic data.

To link the 3D models to the stick models, you must modify the **Dressup** feature. To do this, double-click on **Dressup.1** in the specification tree. The Mechanism Dressup dialog box opens as shown in Figure 7–8.

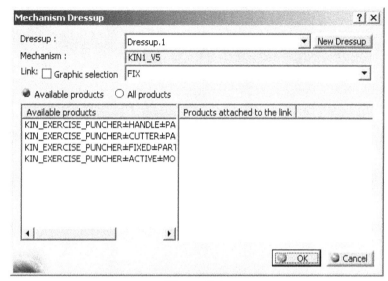

Figure 7–8

Select a V4 stick model in the Link drop-down list and select the corresponding model(s) in the Available products list. Once selected, they are added to the Products attached to the Link list.

Now that the 3D models have been linked to the V4 stick models, the mechanism can be simulated so that the 3D models move with the V4 stick models.

Practice 7a | Converting Assembly Constraints I

Practice Objective

*   Automatically convert assembly constraints into a kinematics mechanism.

In this practice, you will automatically convert the assembly constraints created in the Assembly Design workbench into kinematic joints to quickly simulate an assembly.

Task 1 - Open Excavator.CATProduct.

1. Open **Excavator.CATProduct**. The assembly displays as shown in Figure 7–9.

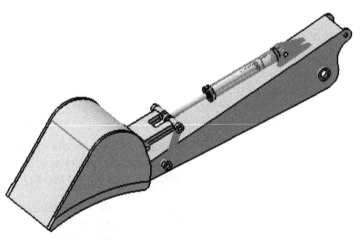

Figure 7–9

The assembly consists of seven components. The intent of the mechanism is to convert the translational motion of the hydraulic cylinder to move the bucket up and down.

Task 2 - Begin the constraint conversion and create a new mechanism.

1. In the DMU Kinematics toolbar, click 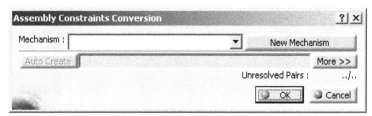 (Assembly Constraints Conversion). The Assembly Constraints Conversion dialog box opens as shown in Figure 7–10.

Figure 7–10

2. Click **New Mechanism** and accept the default name of **Mechanism.1**. The Assembly Constraints Conversion dialog box reports that there are 11 unresolved pairs.

3. To convert the constraints of the assembly into joints, click **Auto Create**. The system analyzes the constraints for each model and creates a corresponding joint.

   For example, the **Stick** component has a Fix constraint and automatically becomes the fixed part in the mechanism.

4. Once complete, the Assembly Constraints dialog box should report that there are no unresolved pairs, as shown in Figure 7–11. Click **OK** to continue.

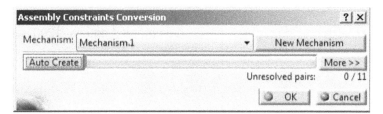

Figure 7–11

5. In the specification tree, expand the **Mechanisms** branch. The mechanism has 1 DOF, as shown in Figure 7–12.

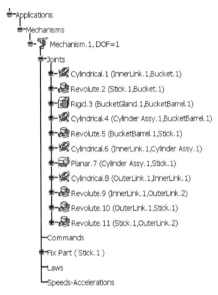

Figure 7–12

6. To constrain the remaining degree of freedom, a command will be added to move the hydraulic cylinder. The motion of the rod in the cylinder is controlled by **Cylindrical.4**. Edit this joint to be **Length driven.**

Task 3 - Simulate the mechanism.

1. Perform a simulation that moves *Command.1* between **150** and **-1200**. The resting position of the model when *Command.1* equals -1200 is shown in Figure 7–13.

Figure 7–13

2. Save the model and close the window.

Practice 7b	# Convert Assembly Constraints II

Practice Objective

- Manually convert assembly constraints into a kinematics mechanism.

In this practice, you will manually convert assembly constraints into joints. Depending on how a designer defines assembly constraints between components, the automatic conversion might not always produce the required results. By manually converting the constraints, you are able to interact with the system to correctly determine which joints should be added to the mechanism.

Task 1 - Open Bore-Device-Assembled.CATProduct.

1. Open **Bore-Device-Assembled.CATProduct**. The assembly displays as shown in Figure 7–14.

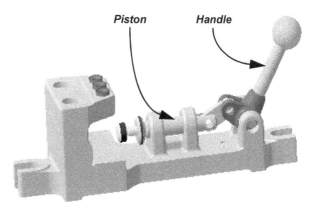

Piston   *Handle*

Figure 7–14

The assembly consists of 12 components. The intent of the mechanism is to convert the rotation motion of moving the handle, into the translation motion of the piston arrangement. A number of these components will remain fixed in the mechanism.

Task 2 - Begin constraint conversion and create a new mechanism.

1. In the DMU Kinematics toolbar, click 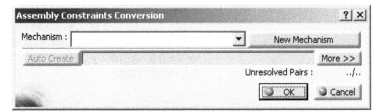 (Assembly Constraints Conversion). The Assembly Constraints Conversion dialog box opens as shown in Figure 7–15.

Figure 7–15

2. Click **New Mechanism** and accept the default name of **Mechanism.1**.

3. Click **More**. The Assembly Constraints Conversion dialog box expands, as shown in Figure 7–16.

Components involved in constraints

Constraint conversion to joints

Fixed part definition

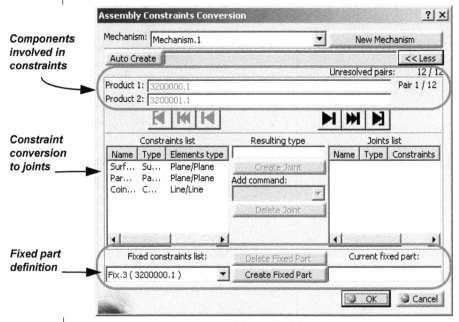

Figure 7–16

The *Fixed part definition* area is at the bottom of the dialog box. The system locates any model with a fix constraint and adds it to the Fix Constraints List.

4. Expand the Fixed Constraints List drop-down list. Note that only one model displays in the list. Select this model.

5. Click **Create Fixed Part**. The **3200000.1** model is moved to the *Current fixed part* field.

Task 3 - Convert assembly constraints to kinematic joints.

In this task, you will step through each pair of models in the assembly and select to convert the constraints for this pair into a joint. By listing the constraints created between a pair, the system can identify possible joint solutions. For example, if an axial coincidence is detected, it can be converted to a cylindrical constraint.

If a model has been constrained in six degrees of freedom, a **Rigid** joint can be created. However, when assembling components, such as a cylindrical pin, the rotational degree of freedom about the axis of the cylinder is often left unconstrained. In this case, the system will not be able to create a rigid constraint. The rigid constraint will need to be defined manually.

1. The current pair consists of **3200000** (fixed part) and **3200001**, which should be rigidly constrained. Select the three constraints under *Constraints List* using <Shift>, as shown in Figure 7–17. As you select each constraint, the possible joint shown in the *Resulting type* field updates.

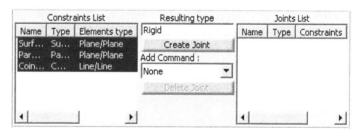

Figure 7–17

2. With all three constraints selected, a **Rigid** joint can be created. Click **Create Joint**. The constraints for this pair are converted to a **Rigid.1** joint in the *Joints List* field, as shown in Figure 7–18.

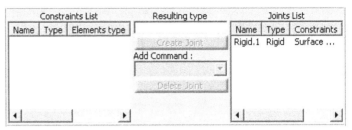

Figure 7–18

3. Click 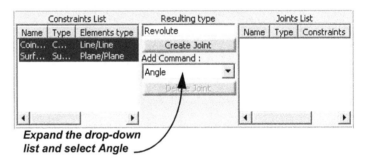 to step forward to the next pair. The next pair under consideration is **3200000** (fixed part) and **3200002**. A commanded **Revolute** joint is required between these two components.

4. Select the two constraints using <Shift>.

5. Expand the Add Command drop-down list and select **Angle** as shown in Figure 7–19.

Expand the drop-down list and select Angle

Figure 7–19

6. Click **Create Joint**. **Revolute.2** is added to the Joints list.

7. Click to step forward to the unresolved pair of **3200000** and **3200006**.

8. Create a **Prismatic** joint (**Prismatic.3**) using the available constraints.

9. Step forward to the pair of **3200001** and **3200003**. This pair consists of a **Block** and **Pin** that should be fixed in the mechanism.

10. Select the two available constraints. Since the **Pin** model was not constrained to rotate along its axis, the resulting joint type is **Revolute**. There is no way to create a **Rigid** joint for this model pair.

11. Click ▶| to move to the next pair. The **Rigid** joint will be created outside the Assembly Constraints Conversion dialog box.

12. Convert the remaining constraints in the model to kinematic joints, as follows:

Pair	Product 1	Product 2	Action
5/12	3200001.1	3200003.2	Click ▶| to skip.
6/12	3200001.1	3200003.3	Click ▶| to skip.
7/12	3200002.1	3200004.1	Click ▶| to skip.
8/12	3200002.1	3200007.1	Cylindrical
9/12	3200004.1	3200005.1	Click ▶| to skip.
10/12	3200006.1	3200007.1	Revolute
11/12	3200006.1	3200009.1	Click ▶| to skip.

13. The last pair, **3200008.1** and **3200009.1**, should also be skipped. Seven unresolved pairs should remain. Click **OK** to close the Assembly Constraints Conversion dialog box.

Task 4 - Simulate the mechanism.

1. In the specification tree, expand the **Applications> Mechanisms** branch. **Mechanism.1** has zero degrees of freedom and can be simulated.

2. Click 🖱.

3. Select **Immediate** and drag the slider for *Command.1*. The mechanism will update with the new angle value. Note that the handle and other models are not moving with the simulation. Although the mechanism can be simulated, it has not been completed as defined with respect to the design intent.

4. Reset the simulation and close the Kinematics Simulation dialog box.

Task 5 - Create Rigid joints and simulate the mechanism.

1. Create four Rigid joints between the models listed in the table below. After each joint, the system will inform you that the mechanism can be simulated.

Part 1	Part 2
3200002.1	3200004.1
3200004.1	3200005.1
3200009.1	3200006.1
3200008.1	3200009.1

2. Simulate the mechanism using (Simulation with Commands). Move the mechanism through a range of motion to ensure that all of the joints function correctly.

3. Save the model and close the window.

Practice 7c

(Optional) Converting V4 Assemblies

Practice Objective

- Replay V4 Kinematic mechanisms in V5.

Task 1 - Open V4 Puncher.CATProduct.

1. Open **V4_Puncher.CATProduct**. The assembly displays as shown in Figure 7–20.

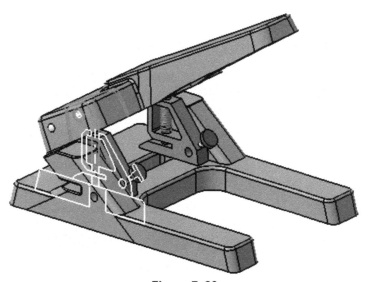

Figure 7–20

The assembly consists of three V4 3D models (handle, cutter, and fixed part) that have been added to the V5 product. Additionally, there is a fourth 2D model (active model) that contains the V4 kinematic data.

2. Expand the last model in the specification tree, **KIN_EXERCISE_PUNCHER+ACTIVE+MODEL+KIN+DEFI NED**, as shown in Figure 7–21.

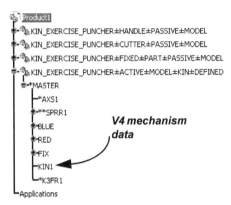

Figure 7–21

KIN1 is the V4 mechanism that will be transferred to V5 in this practice.

Task 2 - Copy and Paste the kinematic data.

1. Right-click on **KIN1** and select **Copy**.

2. Right-click on Applications and select **Paste**. A Conversion Information window opens as shown in Figure 7–22.

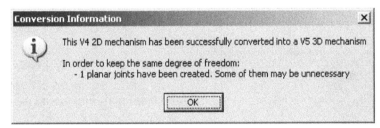

Figure 7–22

3. Click **OK**.

4. Expand the Applications entry. Two dressups and one mechanism have been added to the tree.

5. Expand **Dressup.1**. Note that it lists **KIN1_V5** as the mechanism to which the dressups apply.

Task 3 - Simulate the V4 mechanism.

1. Click 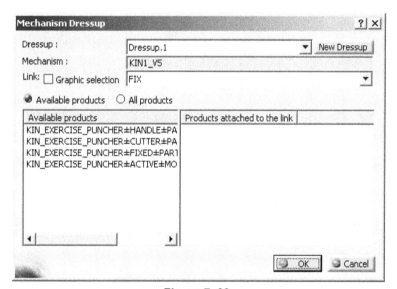 (Simulation with Commands) and verify that **KIN1_V5** is listed in the Mechanism drop-down list.

2. Select **On request** and enter a *Command.1* value of **13**.

3. Play the simulation. Only the stick models in the V4 mechanism are moving. This is because the 3D models have not been linked to the V4 stick models.

4. Click **Reset** and close the Kinematics Simulation dialog box.

Task 4 - Assign a V5 model to each V4 2D component.

1. In the specification tree, double-click on **Dressup.1.** The Mechanism Dressup dialog box opens as shown in Figure 7–23.

Figure 7–23

To link a V5 model to a V4 set, select the V4 set in the Link drop-down list and select the corresponding V5 model in the Available products list.

2. Assign each V4 2D component to a part in the assembly, as follows:

V4 Set	Assembly Part
FIX	KIN_EXERCISE_PUNCHER±FIXED±PART±PASSIVE±MODEL.1
BLUE	KIN_EXERCISE_PUNCHER±HANDLE±PASSIVE±MODEL.1
RED	KIN_EXERCISE_PUNCHER±CUTTER±PASSIVE±MODEL.1

3. Click **OK** to complete the operation.

Task 5 - Simulate the mechanism.

1. Click ⊚ (Simulation with Commands) and verify that **KIN1_V5** is listed in the Mechanism drop-down list.

2. Select **On request** and enter a *Command.1* value of **13**.

3. Play the simulation.

4. Orient the model into the Front saved view, using ⬛ (Front View).

5. Replay the simulation. Note the translation of the red model (**KIN_EXERCISE_PUNCHER±CUTTER±PASSIVE±MODEL.1**). Does it travel deep enough to punch a hole in the paper?

6. Close all of the dialog boxes.

7. Save the model and close the window.

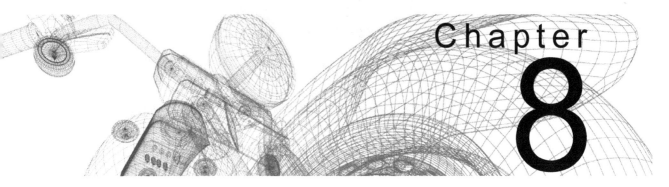

Chapter 8

Laws in ENOVIA DMU

Laws enable you to create relationships between multiple commands in a mechanism. If more than one command exists, they can be related to a command. Consequently, the entire mechanism can be driven by modifying the value of a single command.

Learning Objectives in this Chapter

- Learn to control simulations with Laws in ENOVIA DMU.
- Use 2D Curves to control simulations.

8.1 Simulation with Laws in ENOVIA DMU

If more than one command exists in a mechanism, all of the commands are manually modified to achieve the required motion. When a mechanism is simulated in this way, the commands can move at the same time but are not linked to each other.

Using model parameters and formulas, you can control a mechanism based on a change in time. When a mechanism is created, a KINTime parameter is created in the mechanism. This parameter can be assigned a value (in hours, minutes, or seconds), which represents the total amount of time required to move the mechanism. By relating the KINTime parameter for the commands of a mechanism using formulas, it is possible to control multiple commands with respect to time.

For example, a kinematic model of an analog clock would require a KINTime parameter of 12 hours. This would be the time required for the hour hand to travel around once and the minute hand to travel around twelve times.

General Steps

Use the following general steps to drive a mechanism using the KINTime parameter:

1. Assign a formula to each command parameter.
2. Assign a range to the KINTime parameter.
3. Simulate the mechanism.

Step 1 - Assign a formula to each command parameter.

For the simulation to be driven by time, you must relate the command(s) for the mechanism to the KINTime parameter. This is accomplished by adding formulas for each command.

Expand the **Applications>Mechanisms>Mechanism.1> Commands** branch in the specification tree to display the available commands for the mechanism, as shown in Figure 8–1.

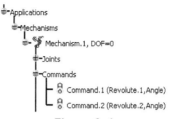

Figure 8–1

Edit the command by double-clicking on it. This opens the Command Edition dialog box. Right-click in the *Command value* field and select **Edit Formula**, as shown in Figure 8–2.

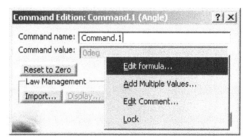

Figure 8–2

The Formula Editor dialog box opens. To display the mechanism specific parameters, as shown in Figure 8–3, select the mechanism in the specification tree.

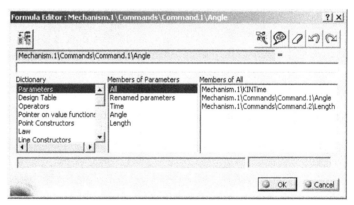

Figure 8–3

Formulas used to drive command parameters with respect to KINTime typically have the following syntax:

Command Parameter = (KINTime / Total Time) * Distance

Where:

Total Time = the *Maximum Bound* value of the KINTime range.

Distance = the total length or angle travelled by the commanded joint.

Enter the formula as defined by the current mechanism into the field provided. Once all of the commands have been related to the KINTime parameter, the range for the KINTime parameter can be assigned.

Step 2 - Assign a range to the KINTime parameter.

When the KINTime parameter is used to drive the commands of a mechanism, the **Simulation with Laws** tool must be used.

To access the KINTime parameter, click (Simulation with Laws) in the Simulation flyout in the DMU Kinematics toolbar. The Kinematics Simulation dialog box opens as shown in Figure 8–4. This dialog box is similar to the **Simulation with Commands** tool. However, the only adjustable input is the KINTime parameter.

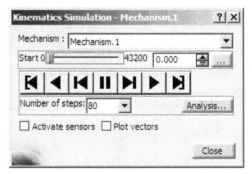

Figure 8–4

To assign a range to the KINTime parameter, click 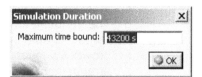. The Simulation Duration dialog box opens as shown in Figure 8–5. Enter a value for the *Maximum time bound* as defined by the current mechanism. Use the following units: Seconds = s, Minutes = min, and Hours = h.

Simulation Duration

Maximum time bound: 43200 s

OK

Figure 8–5

Click **OK** to complete the operation. Leave the Kinematics Simulation dialog box open for the next step.

Step 3 - Simulate the mechanism.

Specify an end time by moving the slider or entering a value.

Click ▶ to play the simulation.

Similar to the **Simulation with Commands** tool, the value entered for the *Number of steps* controls the speed at which the mechanism is going to move. A small number of steps causes the mechanism to move quickly and a large number of steps causes the mechanism to slow down.

8.2 Using 2D Curves

Commands are used to drive a mechanism. For example, an **Angle** command moves a **Revolute** joint and a **Length** command moves a **Prismatic** joint. Typically, values for commands are entered manually to simulate the mechanism.

The 2D curve functionality enables you to drive a command with respect to time though the use of a sketch or text file. This provides a much faster method of defining complex command arrangements for a simulation.

General Steps

Use the following general steps to drive a command using a 2D curve or text file:

1. Define the input data.
2. Edit the command.
3. Simulate the mechanism.

Step 1 - Define the input data.

A kinematic law can drive a command using a sketch or text file.

Sketch

The 2D sketch defines a graph that is used to control the command. The X-axis of the graph defines time, while the Y-axis defines the value of the command. The origin of the sketch denotes the (0,0) value. An example is shown in Figure 8–6. The units for the command value are dependent on the type of command being driven (degrees for an angle-driven joint and millimeters, or other length units, for a length-driven joint).

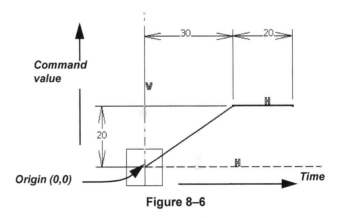

Figure 8–6

Therefore, at t=0 the command would have a value of 0 mm. This value would increase to 20 mm at t=30 and remain in this position until t=50, which would indicate the end of the simulation.

This sketch can be created in any part model in the mechanism. However, creating a separate part model that contains all of the kinematic laws aids in better organization of the assembly specification tree.

Text File

If you do not have access to a Part Design or Generative Shape Design license, kinematic laws can also be driven through a text file. The file should contain at least two columns: *Time* and *Command value*. An example is shown in Figure 8–7. This example produces the same results as the sketch shown in Figure 8–6.

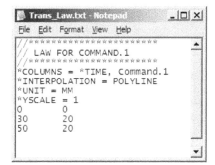

Figure 8–7

The text file uses a specific structure that is described as follows:

Option	Description
Comments	The first three lines in the text file shown in Figure 8–7 are commented by adding // at the start of the lines.
Columns	The Columns line indicates the value of the columns of the table. In this case, the first column is the Time parameter, while the second column indicates the value of *Command.1*.
Interpolation	The points of the table can be joined using a spline or polyline.
Unit	Indicates the unit of measurement for the values of the command. In this case, the command is length-driven, with the units in millimeters.
Yscale	Enter a scale value to increase the command value. For example, if a scale of 10 were used, the command value would range from **0** to **200 mm**.

One advantage of using a text file is that you can define a law for more than one command at a time. To do this, add a column to the table and fill in the appropriate column, interpolation, unit, and yscale information. The text file example shown in Figure 8–8 drives two commands named **Prismatic** and **Revolute**.

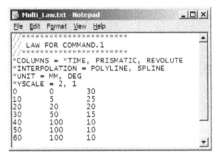

Figure 8–8

Step 2 - Edit the command.

To associate a law with a command, double-click on the command in the specification tree. The Command Edition dialog box opens as shown in Figure 8–9. The options are described in

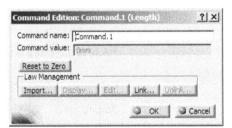

Figure 8–9

Sketch

To link a sketch to the command, click **Link** in the Command Edition dialog box. The Sketch Selection dialog box opens as shown in Figure 8–10.

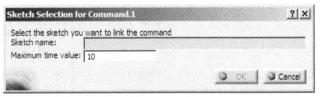

Figure 8–10

To define the Sketch name, select the sketch in the model or specification tree. Enter a *Maximum time* value that corresponds to the time defined in the sketch. For example, if the overall length of the sketch is 50 mm, enter **50**. If a different number is entered, the sketch is scaled along the horizontal axis.

Once complete, click **OK**. The system prompts you that the law has been successfully created, as shown in Figure 8–11.

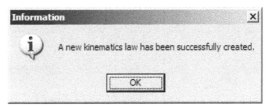

Figure 8–11

The system automatically creates a law feature in the model that contains the sketch. This law feature also displays in the specification tree. The law evaluates the command values based on the sketch. The data is then related to the command value using the formula in the law branch of the mechanism, as shown in Figure 8–12.

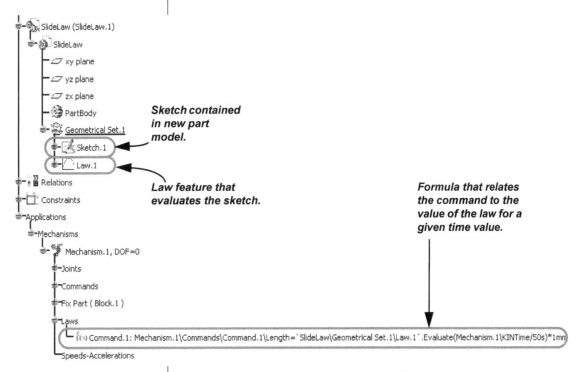

Figure 8–12

Text File

To link a text file to a command, click **Import** in the Command Edition dialog box. The File Selection dialog box opens, enabling you to browse for the text file. Once you select a text file, the Import File Laws Result dialog box opens as shown in Figure 8–13. This dialog box reports the commands that are driven by the law.

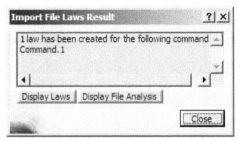

Figure 8–13

Click **Display Laws** to display a graph of the law. You can also click **Display File Analysis** to open a window that helps you to debug any errors in the text file, as shown in Figure 8–14.

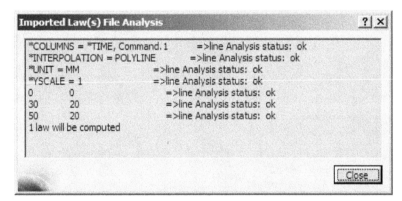

Figure 8–14

The system creates a new part model in the assembly that contains a sketch and law feature, as shown in Figure 8–15. The sketch is based on the data in the text file. Each line in the file becomes the X- and Y-coordinates for a point in the sketch. These points are connected with lines (if the polyline option is used) or splines. A law is generated to extract information from the sketch and a formula links the law to the command.

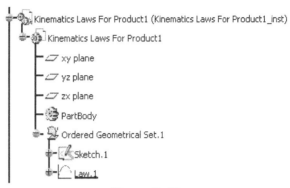

Figure 8–15

This import is not associative and changes to the text file do not update in the mechanism. To modify the law, you must modify the sketch.

Editing the Command

At any time, you can edit the command to display the **Law Management** options. You can edit the command using the Command Edition dialog box. The options in this dialog box consist of **Import** and **Link**, and the three additional options described as follows:

Option	Description
Display	Displays a graph of the law driving the current command.
Edit	Opens the sketch feature driving the command in the Sketcher workbench for editing. This option requires a Part Design or Generative Shape Design license.
Unlink	Removes the law that is currently driving the command. This can be used to unlink a sketch or text file.

Step 3 - Simulate the mechanism.

With the command defined, the mechanism can now be simulated. Click ⚙ (Simulation) in the DMU Generic Animation toolbar and select the mechanism to be simulated. The system opens the Edit Simulation and Kinematics Simulation dialog boxes.

Select the *Use Laws* tab in the Kinematics Simulation dialog box, as shown in Figure 8–16. This enables you to modify the time value to simulate the mechanism based on the laws that have been defined.

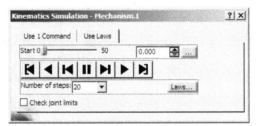

Figure 8–16

The **Automatic Insert** option in the Edit Simulation dialog box can be used to record each step in the simulation. For example, if the simulation has a time duration of 50 seconds, set the number of steps to 50 and enable the **Automatic Insert** option to record the mechanism positions for each second in the simulation. Click ▶ to run the simulation and begin the automatic insertion process.

Practice 8a	# Laws - ENOVIA DMU

Practice Objectives

- Relate commands to time using formulas.
- Run a simulation with laws.

In this practice, you will simulate the motion of a puncher in the ENOVIA DMU Kinematics workbench. The joints have already been created for the mechanism. The command for each joint will be related to time using formulas. The puncher will be commanded to turn 65 degrees and the box will be commanded to move 100mm toward the puncher. Both of these motions will be completed in 100 seconds. The goal of the practice is to have the box positioned directly beneath the puncher at the precise moment that it reaches the extent of its rotation.

Task 1 - Open Punch.CATProduct.

1. Open **Punch.CATProduct**. The model displays as shown in Figure 8–17. The assembly consists of the following parts: **Support**, **Puncher**, and **Box**.

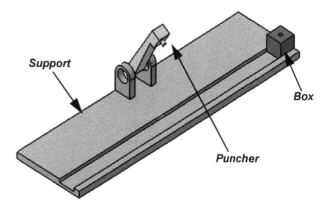

Figure 8–17

2. Select **Analyze>Mechanism Analysis**. The Mechanism Analysis dialog box opens.

3. Investigate the two joints by selecting them in the list. Only the models involved in the joint are highlighted on the screen. **Revolute.1** and **Command.1** rotate the **Puncher** model, while **Prismatic.1** and **Command.2** translate the **Box**.

4. Close the Mechanism Analysis dialog box.

Task 2 - Apply a formula to the Puncher command.

In this task, you will apply a formula to control the value of *Command.1* with respect to the KINTime parameter. This enables the movements calculated by the simulation to be reported with respect to time.

1. Expand the following branches in the specification tree: **Applications>Mechanisms>Mechanism.1>Commands**. Two commands display as shown in Figure 8–18.

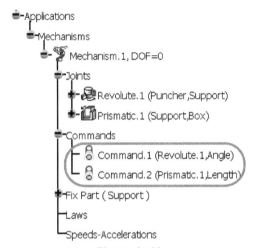

Figure 8–18

2. To control the command for the puncher, double-click on **Command.1**. The Command Edition dialog box opens.

3. Right-click in the *Command value* field and select **Edit Formula**, as shown in Figure 8–19.

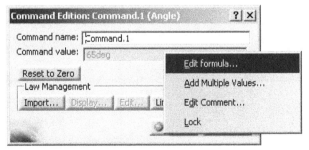

Figure 8–19

4. The Formula Editor dialog box opens. This dialog box displays all of the parameters that exist in the model. To display only the parameters relative to the mechanism, select **Mechanism.1** in the specification tree. The Formula Editor opens as shown in Figure 8–20.

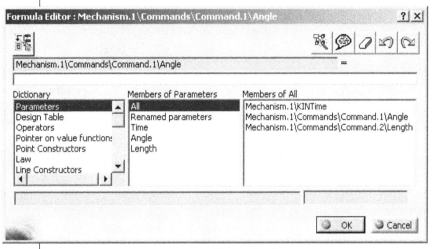

Figure 8–20

Design Considerations

The KINtime parameter, representing kinematic time, controls the movements of the joints using real time. For example, you will use this parameter to control the angular position of the puncher with respect to time. The puncher will begin at a start angle of 65 degrees and rotate downward to an angle of 0 degrees over 100 seconds. The formula for this command is shown in Figure 8–21.

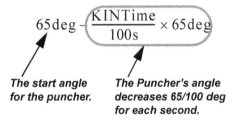

$$65\text{deg} - \left(\frac{\text{KINTime}}{100\text{s}} \times 65\text{deg} \right)$$

The start angle for the puncher. *The Puncher's angle decreases 65/100 deg for each second.*

Figure 8–21

5. In the Formula Editor dialog box, enter **65deg-**.

6. Double-click on **Mechanism.1\KINTime** to add it to the field above.

7. Complete the formula by entering **/ 100s * 65deg** so that the Formula Editor dialog box opens as shown in Figure 8–22.

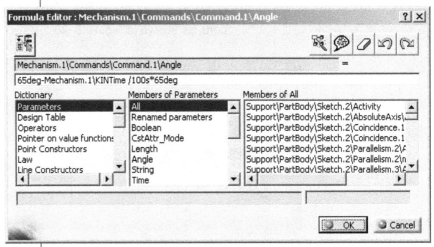

Figure 8–22

Based on this formula:

- When KINTime = 0s, the puncher will be at 65deg.
- When KINTime = 100s, the puncher will be at 0deg.

8. Click **OK** twice to close the dialog boxes.

Task 3 - Apply a formula to the box command parameter.

Design Considerations

You will use the same type of formula to control the position of the box. In this case, the box will begin at its current location and translate 100mm over 100 seconds. At the end of the motion, the box will be positioned directly beneath the puncher. The formula for this command is shown in Figure 8–23. For each second, the box will translate 1mm (100/100 = 1).

$$\frac{\text{KINTime}}{100s} \times 100\text{mm}$$

Figure 8–23

1. Edit **Command.2** and enter the following formula: **Mechanism.1\KINTime / 100s *100mm**. The Formula Editor opens as shown in Figure 8–24.

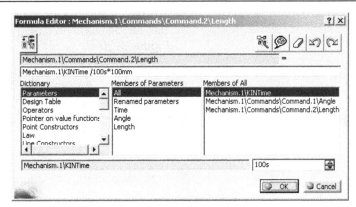

Figure 8–24

Based on this formula:

- When KINTime = 0s, the box will be at current location.
- When KINTime = 100s, the box will move 100mm.

2. Click **OK** twice to close the dialog boxes.

Task 4 - Play the mechanism with laws.

In this task, you will simulate the mechanism. Since formulas have been used to relate the mechanism commands to the KINTime parameter, the **Simulation with Laws** tool must be used.

1. In the DMU Kinematics toolbar, expand the Simulation flyout, and click (Simulation with Laws). The Kinematics Simulation dialog box opens as shown in Figure 8–25.

*Note that the only parameter that can be controlled by the **Simulation with Laws** tool is time.*

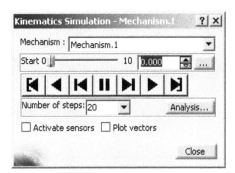

Figure 8–25

2. To specify a range for the KINTime parameter, click **....** The Simulation Duration dialog box opens as shown in Figure 8–26.

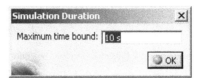

Figure 8–26

3. In the *Maximum time bound* field, enter **100s** and click **OK**.

4. Expand the Number of steps drop-down list, and select **80**.

5. Click ▶ to simulate the mechanism.

6. Once the simulation is complete, close the dialog box.

Note that the simulation takes less than 100 seconds to complete. Although the simulation calculates positions and other measures with respect to time, CATIA will display a simulation based on the number of steps assigned. Each step can take more or less than 1 second based on the processor speed. Do not be concerned with the true duration of the simulation. The only duration that matters is the simulation time of the analysis, which has been set to 100 seconds.

7. Save the model and close the window.

Practice 8b

Using 2D Curves

Practice Objectives

- Create DMU Kinematic laws.
- Simulate with laws.
- Compile a simulation.

In this practice, you will simulate the closing of a hard top convertible roof. The goal is to ensure that the roof can completely close in 20 seconds. To incorporate this time component into the analysis, you will drive the simulation through laws that use a 2D curve. You will explore the two methods of assigning a law to a command: sketch and text file.

This simulation can also be performed without using a kinematic law, by manually positioning the commands and recording joint positions for each of the 20 seconds in the analysis. However, using laws that use a 2D curve provides a more efficient method of controlling multiple commands with respect to time.

Joints and commands have already been established in the assembly. In addition, the 2D curve data (a sketch and a text file) for the law creation has also been created. The assembly displays as shown in Figure 8–27.

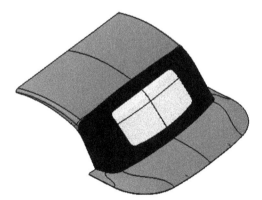

Figure 8–27

Task 1 - Open a product model.

1. Select **File>Open**. In the *Roof* folder, select **RetractableHardtop.CATProduct**.

2. Review the components in the specification tree, as shown in Figure 8–28. The **Roof**, **CPillar**, and **CompartmentLid** components move during the simulation. First the **ComponentLid** opens, and then the **Roof** and **CPillar** rotate and translate. Finally, the **ComponentLid** closes.

Figure 8–28

Task 2 - Investigate the mechanism.

In this task, you will review the kinematic mechanism that has already been created in the assembly.

1. In the specification tree, expand the **Applications** branch and review the contents of the **Joints** and **Commands** nodes. The specification tree displays as shown in Figure 8–29.

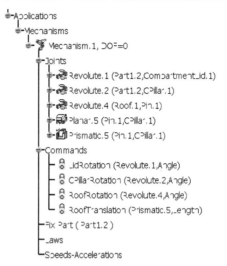

Figure 8–29

2. In the DMU Kinematics toolbar, click (Simulation with Commands) to better understand the function of each joint and command. The Kinematics Simulation dialog box opens as shown in Figure 8–30.

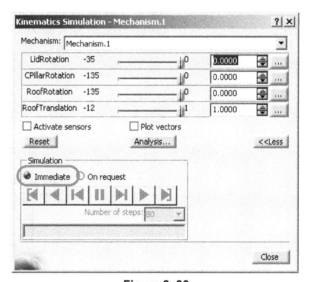

Figure 8–30

3. In the Kinematics Simulation dialog box, verify that the **Immediate** option is selected.

4. To investigate the motion of each command, drag each of the four sliders back and forth. The system simulates each command to visualize the range of motion for each joint.

5. When you have finished, click **Reset** in the Kinematics Simulation dialog box. The mechanism returns to its assembled position.

6. Close the dialog box.

Task 3 - Associating a 2D curve to a kinematic law.

In this task, you will link a kinematic law to a command to define the command value through the duration of the simulation. The first method used to create a law is based on a 2D curve. The 2D curve has been created as the **LidLawCurve** sketch and controls the **LidRotation** command.

1. Show the **Law** component. It consists of a sketch that defines the angular rotation of the **LidRotation** command.

Design Considerations

The sketch in the **Law** component is used to drive the lid rotation. The X-axis of the sketch defines the time duration (in this case, 20 seconds), while the Y-axis defines the command value. The lid rotates from 0 to 45 degrees over 8 seconds, remains open for 4 seconds, and closes over another 8 seconds, as shown in Figure 8–31.

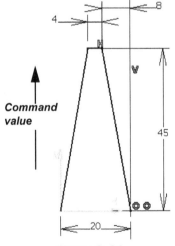

Figure 8–31

2. In the specification tree, expand the **Commands** branch and double-click on **LidRotation**. The Command Edition dialog box opens as shown in Figure 8–32.

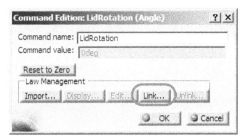

Figure 8–32

3. In the Command Edition dialog box, click **Link**. The Sketch Selection dialog box opens as shown in Figure 8–33.

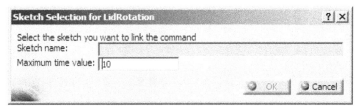

Figure 8–33

4. In the specification tree, expand the **Law** component. Under **Geometrical Set.1**, select the **LidLawCurve** sketch as shown in Figure 8–34. The selected sketch displays in the Sketch Selection dialog box.

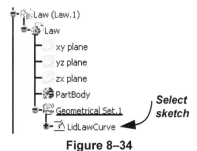

Figure 8–34

5. For the *Maximum time* value, enter **20**. This is the required time duration for the simulation. The Command Edition and Sketch Selection dialog boxes are shown in Figure 8–35.

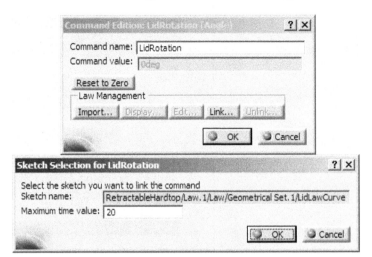

Figure 8–35

6. In the Sketch Selection dialog box, click **OK**. The system indicates that the law was created successfully, as shown in Figure 8–36.

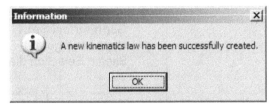

Figure 8–36

7. Click **OK**. In the Command Edition dialog box, click **Display**. This opens a separate window in which the law curve displays, as shown in Figure 8–37.

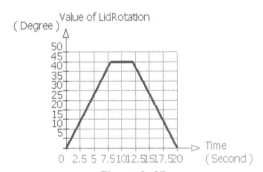

Figure 8–37

8. Close the Laws Display window. Click **OK** in the Command Edition dialog box to finish creating the law.

9. In the specification tree, under the **Mechanisms** branch, expand **Laws**. A formula was automatically created linking the law and command.

Task 4 - Simulate with laws.

In this task, you will create a temporary simulation so that you can review the motion prescribed by the law. Once complete, this simulation is cancelled so that the kinematic assembly can be further defined.

1. In the DMU Generic Animation toolbar, click

   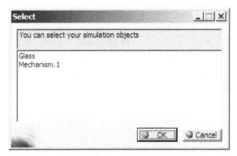 (Simulation). The Select dialog box opens as shown in Figure 8–38.

Figure 8–38

2. Double-click on **Mechanism.1**. The Kinematics Simulation and Edit Simulation dialog boxes open.

3. In the Kinematics Simulation dialog box, select the *Use Laws* tab as shown in Figure 8–39.

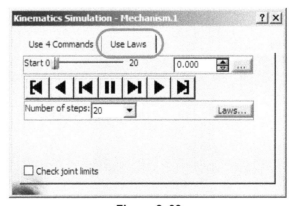

Figure 8–39

Design Considerations

4. Ensure that the *Number of steps* is set to **20** and click ▶ in the Kinematics Simulation dialog box.

With the number of steps set to 20, the system creates a step for each second in the simulation. During the simulation, the **Lid** component rotates to its maximum opening, remains stationary (while the rest of the roof retracts into place), and then closes.

5. In the Edit Simulation dialog box, click **Cancel**. You must define additional laws before completing the simulation.

Task 5 - Create laws by importing a text file.

Another way to create a law is to import information from a text file. The text file must be set to tell CATIA which joints are driven by the law, and the joint position at each given time interval. This is an excellent method of creating multiple laws at once. In task you will create three laws based on the information imported by the text file.

A text file has been created for you that includes information about joint positions at various time intervals. The contents of the text file are shown in Figure 8–40. The command names in the text file match three of the commands in the specification tree.

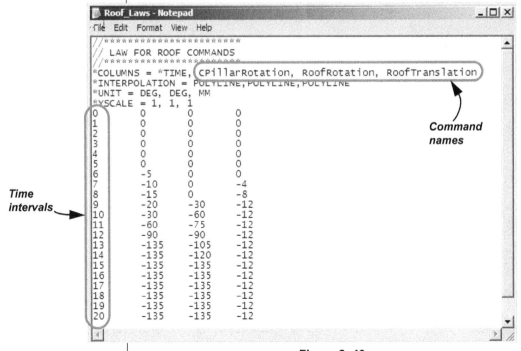

Figure 8–40

1. In the specification tree, in the **Commands** branch, double-click on **CPillarRotation**.

2. In the Command Edition dialog box, click **Import**.

3. In the File Selection dialog box, double-click on **Roof_Laws.txt**. The Import File Laws Result dialog box opens as shown in Figure 8–41.

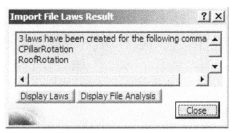

Figure 8–41

4. Click **Display Laws** to display a graphical representation of the imported laws. The laws display as shown in Figure 8–42.

For multiple laws, select a command from the legend on the right side to display the correct range of values.

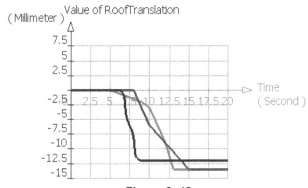

Figure 8–42

5. Close the Laws Display window.

6. Click **Display File Analysis** to display the imported text file. The Law Analysis opens as shown in Figure 8–43.

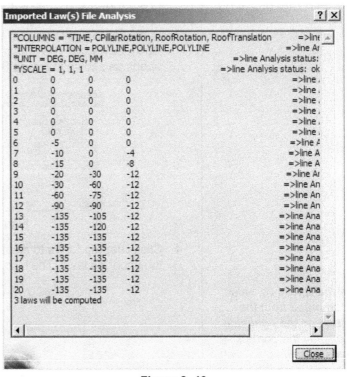

Figure 8–43

7. Close the Imported Law File Analysis dialog box and the Import File Laws Result dialog box.

8. Click **OK** in the Command Edition dialog box.

9. Expand the **Laws** branch in the **Mechanism** and note the formulas that have been added to the specification tree, as shown in Figure 8–44.

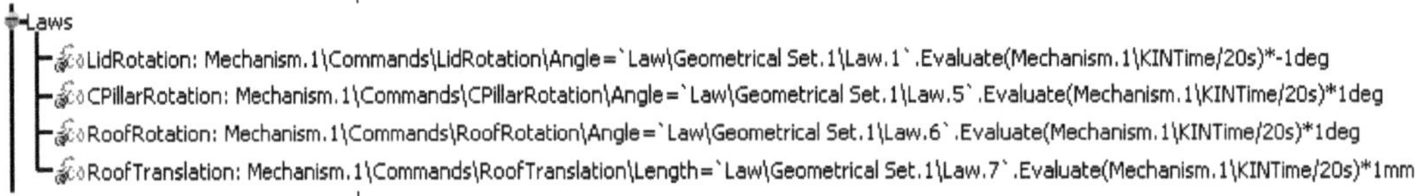

┬Laws
├─ ⚙ LidRotation: Mechanism.1\Commands\LidRotation\Angle=`Law\Geometrical Set.1\Law.1`.Evaluate(Mechanism.1\KINTime/20s)*-1deg
├─ ⚙ CPillarRotation: Mechanism.1\Commands\CPillarRotation\Angle=`Law\Geometrical Set.1\Law.5`.Evaluate(Mechanism.1\KINTime/20s)*1deg
├─ ⚙ RoofRotation: Mechanism.1\Commands\RoofRotation\Angle=`Law\Geometrical Set.1\Law.6`.Evaluate(Mechanism.1\KINTime/20s)*1deg
└─ ⚙ RoofTranslation: Mechanism.1\Commands\RoofTranslation\Length=`Law\Geometrical Set.1\Law.7`.Evaluate(Mechanism.1\KINTime/20s)*1mm

Figure 8–44

10. in the specification tree, expand the **Law** component. Three additional sketches and law features have been added to the geometrical set, as shown in Figure 8–45.

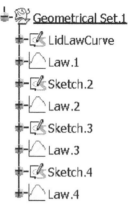

Figure 8–45

Design Considerations

The results of the two laws using 2D curve options are the same. Both the sketch and the imported text file produce a sketch and a corresponding law feature in the specification tree.

Task 6 - Simulate and compile the mechanism.

In this task, you will simulate the mechanism using the laws that have been generated. Since the position of each component has been completely defined throughout the simulation, you will use the **Automatic Insert** option to record each second of the simulation.

1. Click [icon] to simulate the mechanism.

2. Double-click on **Mechanism.1**. The Kinematics Simulation and Edit Simulation dialog boxes open.

3. In the Edit Simulation dialog box, select **Automatic Insert**, as shown in Figure 8–46.

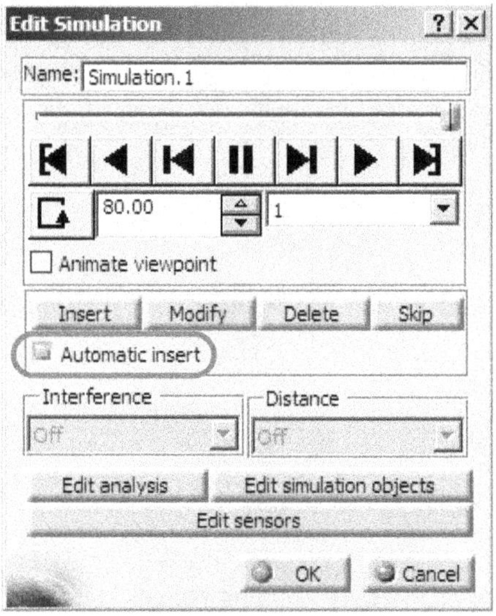

Figure 8–46

4. In the Kinematics Simulation dialog box, select the *Use Laws* tab.

5. For the Number of steps, enter **20**. This coincides with the 20 seconds duration of the simulation.

6. Click ▶ to start the automatic insertion process. The mechanism runs in the background as CATIA creates the simulation.

7. Click **OK** in the Edit Simulation dialog box.

Task 7 - Generate a replay from the simulation.

1. In the DMU Kinematics toolbar, click 🎞 (Compile Simulation). Make the following selections:

   • Select **Generate a replay**.
   • *Simulation name:* **Simulation.1**
   • *Time step:* **0.04**

The Compile Simulation dialog box opens as shown in Figure 8–47.

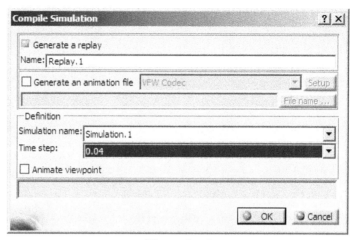

Figure 8–47

2. Click **OK** to create the replay. The system adds a **Replay** branch to the specification tree.

3. Double-click on **Replay.1** to review the simulation.

4. Save and close the file.

www.ingramcontent.com/pod-product-compliance
Lightning Source LLC
Chambersburg PA
CBHW080409060326
40689CB00019B/4185